KANT'S SECOND CRITIQUE
AND THE PROBLEM OF TRANSCENDENTAL ARGUMENTS

KANT'S SECOND CRITIQUE AND THE PROBLEM OF TRANSCENDENTAL ARGUMENTS

ROBERT J. BENTON

MARTINUS NIJHOFF / THE HAGUE / 1977

ISBN 90 247 2055 9

PRINTED IN THE NETHERLANDS

This work is in no way intended as a commentary on the second Critique, or even on the Analytic of that book. Instead I have limited myself to the attempt to extract the essential structure of the argument of the Analytic and to exhibit it as an instance of a transcendental argument (namely, one establishing the conditions of the possibility of a practical cognitive viewpoint). This limitation of scope has caused me, in some cases, to ignore or treat briefly concrete questions of Kant's practical philosophy that deserve much closer consideration; and in other cases it has led me to relegate questions that could not be treated briefly to appendixes, in order not to distract from the development of the argument. As a result, it is the argument-structure itself that receives primary attention, and I think some justification should be offered for this concentration on what may seem to be a purely formal concern.

One of the most common weaknesses of interpretations of Kant's works is a failure to distinguish the level of generality at which Kant's argument is being developed. This failure is particularly fatal in dealing with the Critiques, since in interpreting them it is important to keep clearly in mind that it is not this or that cognition that is at stake, but the possibility of (a certain kind of) knowledge as such. Thus, in interpretations of the second Critique, the transcendental aim of the argument is frequently lost sight of and a more limited ("metaphysical") aim is put in its place for example, justification of the moral law). This conflation of questions that arise on different levels of generality is doubly detrimental. On the one hand, as I try to show in this work, it can lead to failure to understand those aspects of the arguments that are truly transcendental (for example, in the case of the second Critique, the establishing of a practical cognitive viewpoint distinct from the theoretical viewpoint). And, on the other hand, it can contribute to a narrowing of perspective in dealing with a field of cognition once it has been transcendentally established. The latter can be seen in the common tendency to treat Kant's practical philosophy as though

it were solely a moral philosophy, which in turn can lead one to ignore
or misunderstand Kant's numerous writings on political theory. My own
opinion is that the second Critique is concerned with establishing a
cognitive framework within which moral, legal, and political thinking are
all made possible. Thus my limitation of the scope of the present investigation is not intended as a restriction on the area of legitimate concerns
in practical philosophy, but rather as a way of focusing attention on the
prior question of how and in what way practical cognition is possible.
Only after clarity has been attained on that question are we in a position
to raise questions concerning the more concrete concerns of Kant's moral
or political philosophy.

• • •

In quoting passages from the second Critique I have generally made use
of Louis White Beck's translation (copyright © 1956 The Liberal Arts
Press, reprinted by permission of the Bobbs-Merrill Company, Inc.);
but I have made minor changes in the translations throughout, always in
the interest of greater literalness. In cases where the changes are major
I have noted them, but in other cases I have made them silently.

For citing references I have adopted the following method: I cite the
author's last name, the year of publication of the article or book (in the
case of books it is the year of publication of the edition that I used), and
the page number (all three items separated by commas). Complete references are given in the Bibliography. In cases where I make use of only
one work by a given author I sometimes omit the year of publication in
citations, since the year is useful only in distinguishing two works by the
same author. In case an author has two works with the same year of publication, I distinguish them by appending an a, b, etc. to the year.

For references to Kant's works I follow a different scheme: All references to the second Critique are by Academy-edition page number only
(so that when a number appears in parentheses with no other identification
it refers to the second Critique). Other works by Kant are cited by the

following list of abbreviations:

Ethics—*Lectures on Ethics*
GMM—*Groundwork of the Metaphysic of Morals*
KrV—*Critique of Pure Reason*
KU—*Critique of Judgment*
MM—*Metaphysic of Morals*
Religion—*Religion within the Limits of Reason Alone*

Page number references are to the Academy-edition pagination in all cases where those numbers appear in the English texts. In the case of references to the KU I have cited section number rather than page number since there are several commonly available English editions, none of which, I think, have Academy page numbers. In the case of the KrV page numbers, A- and B-edition references are given, rather than Academy-edition numbers, and they are given in the form A111/B222. In all other cases the page numbers are those of the English edition listed in the Bibliography.

Quotations from the *Critique of Pure Reason*, translated by Norman Kemp Smith, copyright © 1929 by Macmillan and Company, Ltd. , are reprinted by permission of St. Martin's Press and Macmillan Co. , Ltd. Quotations from the *Doctrine of Virtue* of the *Metaphysic of Morals*, translated by Mary Gregor, and from the *Groundwork of the Metaphysic of Morals*, translated by H. J. Paton, are reprinted by permission of Harper and Row Publishers, Inc. Quotations from Beck's *Commentary on Kant's Critique of Practical Reason*, copyright © 1960 by the University of Chicago, are reprinted by permission of the University of Chicago Press. Quotations from the *Critique of Judgment*, translated by James Creed Meredith, are reprinted by permission of Oxford University Press.

This work was originally presented as a dissertation submitted to the Graduate Faculty of Political and Social Science of the New School for Social Research in partial fulfillment of the requirements for the degree of Doctor of Philosophy. The first four chapters of the work first appeared, in substantially the same form, in the *Graduate Faculty*

Philosophy Journal, Vol. 6, No. 1 Winter 1977.

. . .

I would like to express my gratitude to Kenley R. Dove for his consistently fruitful criticism and advice; to J. N. Mohanty for invaluable help and encouragement; to Hans Jonas for his critical and helpful suggestions; and to John Wetlaufer for innumerable discussions, during the course of which many of the ideas in this work were first brought to clarity. I would also like to thank Larry Redman for his tireless and repeated typings of the manuscript.

Robert J. Benton

New York, New York
July 1977

CONTENTS

THE PROBLEM OF TRANSCENDENTAL ARGUMENTS AND
THE SECOND CRITIQUE AS TEST CASE   1

1. Introduction   3

2. A Working Model for Transcendental Arguments   7

3. Criteria of a Successful Account of the Argument-
Structure of the Analytic of the Second Critique   20

THE ARGUMENT OF THE ANALYTIC   27

4. Preliminary Outline of the Argument of the Analytic
as a Whole   29

5. The Argument of Chapter 1   36

     The Erklärung and its Remark   38
     Sections 2—4   42
     Sections 5—7   49
     Section 8   53
     The Deduction   55

6. The Argument of Chapter 2   68

     Step 1: The Moral Good Must Be the Supreme Good   70
     Step 2: The Moral Good Can Be the Supreme Good   76

7. The Argument of Chapter 3   87

     The Division of the Chapter   90
     The Moral Feeling   91
     The Moral Interest   97

CONCLUSIONS   103

8. Conclusions and Discussion   105

     The Second Critique   105
     Transcendental Arguments   108

APPENDIXES   113

Appendix A: Beck's Account of the Argument   115
Appendix B: Silber's Account of the Argument   134
Appendix C: The Fact of Pure Practical Reason   145
Appendix D: Maxims and Laws   151

NOTES   165

BIBLIOGRAPHY   169

PART I
THE PROBLEM OF TRANSCENDENTAL
ARGUMENTS AND THE SECOND CRITIQUE
AS TEST CASE

1. INTRODUCTION

Transcendental arguments have been the subject of much discussion in the recent literature. The debate has been of the most radical sort, including strong arguments against the very possibility of transcendental arguments (e. g., Körner, 1967).[1] Others have argued in favor of the possibility of transcendental arguments (e. g., Schaper, 1972). But out of all of this there has arisen no consensus about what a transcendental argument *is* and what its aims are. Moreover, there has been a remarkable lack (especially in the English-language literature) of attempts to establish with any precision or in any detail exactly how a transcendental argument works—what it presupposes and how it must be structured. This lack of consensus on what a transcendental argument is and the near total absence of attempts to specify the structure of such arguments are all the more unfortunate since they would seem to be prerequisites for deciding (or even fruitfully raising) the question of the possibility or impossibility of such arguments.

These difficulties are, I think, tied up with the fact that (again, in the English-language literature) the model for a transcendental argument has implicitly or explicitly been taken as being the deduction in Kant's *Critique of Pure Reason.*[2] That is, most discussions of transcendental arguments (or attempts to construct such arguments) have taken that deduction as their standard of what such an argument must be. The difficulties arise from two interrelated problems that are inherent in this approach: The first is that there is no more agreement about the aims and structure of the deduction in the first Critique than there is about transcendental arguments in general. And the second is that, even in cases where there is some agreement about essential features of the deduction, there is a general lack of clarity about what features of the deduction are attributable to the form of argument as such and what features are attributable to the content and its particular requirements.

The lack of agreement about the aims and structure of the deduction in the first Critique is noteworthy, and it is, of course, aggravated by the fact that Kant completely rewrote the deduction for the second edition: There is not any general agreement about whether one or the other or both editions offer satisfactory arguments, and there is even less agreement about what the argument *is* in either case. But in spite of these disagreements there are two features that *are* generally agreed to be essential to transcendental arguments and that are said to be exemplified in the deduction of the first Critique: These features are a concern with justifying a priori synthetic judgments and an appeal to the conditions of the possibility of experience to ground the argument.

These two features offer the only generally accepted starting point for a discussion of transcendental arguments. Nevertheless, I think that as they are usually understood they are both too general and too specific: They are too general because they do not tell us what a transcendental argument must prove, why it must prove it, or how (by what steps within what structure) it must prove it.[3] From these features we can conclude nothing precise about the structure of a transcendental argument, which is what is needed if we are to be able to discuss such arguments meaningfully.

But these two generally accepted features of transcendental arguments are also too specific, and it is on that fact that my approach to the problem of transcendental arguments is based. In the first place, I think that the interpretation that is usually given to these two features of transcendental arguments is biased by a failure to distinguish what is essential to a transcendental argument as such and what is essential only to the specific argument given in the deduction of the first Critique.

For example, the problem of a priori synthetic judgments has frequently been interpreted as being limited to problems of theoretical judgment (problems of the linking of concept to concept—and this in spite of Kant's reinterpretation of the meaning of a judgment in Section 19 of the deduction); and this tendency has even led, in some cases, to the question's being interpreted as a matter of definitions only (cf. Beck's discussion of this tendency in "Kant's Theory of Definition" and "Can Kant's Synthetic Judgments Be Made Analytic?"—Beck, 1965, 61—98). Likewise, the "conditions of the possibility of experience" can only serve to ground a theoretical argument, since experience is simply a posteriori theoretical knowledge. So in order to establish what a transcendental argument as such is we need to consider the possibility that the generally accepted interpretation has taken as essential some features of the deduction in the first Critique that are really not essential to transcendental arguments as such.

The fact that the generally accepted features of a transcendental argument are too specific also shows up in another way: If we are really to understand transcendental arguments we must have some idea *why* they have the features that they have. Now, it seems to be generally accepted that the transcendental form of argument derives from transcendental philosophy's concern with questions of how certain a priori features of the mind find a content in the world of experience (which, however much it may be itself a product of the mind, always contains elements of bare, factual givenness). But, once again, these questions seem to be generally interpreted according to the model of the deduction in the first Critique. That is, it is assumed that all problems of transcendental philosophy will resolve into problems of how a priori concepts (or "categorial schemata"—cf. Körner, 1967, 318—9), which are themselves purely formal and therefore empty, can be given a content from the side of an object that has grounds outside of the mind. But it is not clear ahead of time that this is the only way that the fundamental problem of transcendental philosophy can appear.

It is my thesis that this explicit or implicit dependence upon the deduction of the first Critique as model for transcendental arguments as such has made it more difficult to see either, in general, what a transcendental argument is, why it is needed, and how it is possible, or, more specifically, precisely what structure such an argument must have.

So in order to answer these questions I propose examining the second Critique rather than the first (and, for the sake of brevity, the Analytic of the second Critique rather than the entire book). And I propose giving a detailed account of that argument in order to provide some solid basis for drawing conclusions about the nature of transcendental arguments.

This project is faced with a double difficulty, however: Not only can we not rely on a generally accepted understanding of transcendental arguments, but we cannot even find agreement about the aims and structure of the argument of the Analytic in the second Critique. Of course, the two problems are not independent: How we understand the transcendental form of argument will determine how we read the second Critique, and vice versa.

To deal with these difficulties I have chosen the following compromise: First (Chapter 2) I propose a hypothetical model of a Kantian transcendental argument, basing the hypothesis on the generally accepted features of such arguments, on selected proposals from the literature, and on certain original interpretations. And, second (Chapter 3), since the hypothesis must be tested against the second Critique, whose argument-structure is itself not generally agreed upon, I propose certain criteria of the success of any interpretation of that argument-structure.

What follows, then (in Chapters 4—7), is an attempt to present the actual argument of the Analytic; this attempt is made in the light of our hypothetical model of a transcendental argument and in keeping with the criteria of success of such an interpretation, but its ultimate guiding principle—and that by which its adequacy must ultimately be judged—is the aim of presenting an account that is both true to the actual wording of the text and that is itself a coherent argument.

In Chapter 8 I sum up the conclusions of this investigation and indicate areas in which further research is needed.

2. A WORKING MODEL FOR TRANSCENDENTAL ARGUMENTS

Since the only generally accepted features of transcendental arguments are the two mentioned above—namely, the establishing of the conditions of the possibility of experience and the justification of a priori synthetic judgments—it is with them that we should begin. We can see in advance that in their commonly accepted form there is some question of their immediate applicability to the second Critique, or, indeed, to any argument other than that of the first Critique.

The first Critique has already explored the conditions of the possibility of experience, and although the account given there might not be exhaustive, it certainly claims to have established the highest principles that are presupposed by experience. Other transcendental arguments might supply further, subsidiary principles, but it would be strange if experience were to turn out to have other, equally important conditions in addition to those developed in the first Critique. More specifically, one result of the first Critique was to show that all our experience must be a strict causal sequence. But within such a strict causal sequence freedom (and therefore moral obligation) could never appear. So even though there might be conditions of the possibility of experience other than those developed in the first Critique, it would seem that those conditions could not include freedom.

Likewise it is not clear how the feature of justifying a priori synthetic judgments applies outside of theoretical knowledge. And the difficulty is made worse by the usual way of discussing the problem, especially among writers on the moral philosophy: Ordinarily the problem is seen as simply one of linking concept to concept (subject to predicate), so that an appeal must be made to some "third thing" to supply a link between the two concepts (see, for example, Beck, 1966, 173; Paton, 1967, 120 n, 128, 213, 244). This way of understanding the problem, of course, has its basis in Kant's own discussion of the question—he even explicitly describes the moral principle as an a priori synthetic judgment in just those terms. But predication seems to be a concern of theoretical knowledge rather than of practical knowledge, and if it is of concern to practical knowledge then we need to see in what way it is of concern. In any case, in the second Critique Kant denies that the moral law can be deduced (47); and, in fact, there seems to be no deduction of an a priori synthetic judgment (in this sense) in the Analytic of the second Critique.

So there are at least some difficulties that stand in the way of any simple use of these two features in interpreting transcendental arguments other than that of the first Critique, and there are serious difficulties with respect to the second Critique. The way around these difficulties would seem to be to generalize the two features in such a way that we can see what their most fundamental basis is. We can then use these generalized formulations in framing the hypothetical model that is to be our guide in interpreting the argument of the second Critique.

There is at least one example in the literature of an attempt to get at the transcendental problem that lies at the root of the feature of establishing the conditions of the possibility of experience: Crawford (making use of a term used by Carnap) proposes to interpret questions of the "conditions of the possibility of experience" more generally as *framework* questions (Crawford, 1963, 265 ff.). On this interpretation, what is established in a transcendental argument is a certain cognitive framework or viewpoint. So, for example, in the first Critique the conditions of the possibility of the theoretical viewpoint as such are established. In particular, establishing the theoretical framework means establishing what theoretical knowledge means, which involves determining, for example, what truth or objectivity mean in a theoretical viewpoint and showing how they are possible. (And so, also, particular questions about the *possibility* of the framework at the same time *presuppose* the framework, but the relation of presupposition is not one of simple logical presupposition since the questions of possibility can only be specificed as questions *within* the framework, but their making the framework possible can only be seen from *outside* the framework.)

The terms "viewpoint" and "framework" indicate metaphorically that what is at stake and what must be accounted for is not simply a set of phenomena but a set of relations of phenomena, a certain set of rules whereby phenomena are brought into systematic unity. Later (Chapter 4) I will introduce Kant's term "realm" (from the third Critique) in this context to indicate that there is, more particularly, a question of the *lawful* relations among phenomena. It will turn out that for Kant, although there is more than one cognitive realm (or viewpoint, or framework), there is only one set of phenomena, namely, the phenomena that appear in experience.

But in any case, even without anticipating Kant's position, Crawford's approach already suggests the possibility that experience—and the theoretical framework in general—is only one framework, and that there might be other viewpoints for which we need to establish the conditions of possibility. In particular, it suggests the possibility of a practical viewpoint that is not just a subset of the theoretical viewpoint but rather a wholly different framework for knowledge.

Before exploring this approach further, we should consider ways in which the second feature of transcendental arguments could be generalized. Henrich makes a suggestion (although it is not immediately linked to the question of a priori synthetic judgments) that gives us a way of understanding what the real basis is of the problem of a priori synthetic judgments. In his account of the argument-structure of the B-edition deduction in the first Critique (Henrich, 1969, 646f., 657f.), he argues that the fundamental problem of synthesis that lies behind the Deduction is not at all limited to the linking of concept to concept. Instead it goes back to the fact that for Kant all our knowledge has two roots—intellect and sensibility—and these two faculties are irreducibly distinct. So, for example, the real problem of a transcendental deduction for theoretical cognition is to show how a synthetic relation between intuitions and concepts (the categories) is possible a priori. Or, more accurately, the problem is to show that the categories are "applicable" a priori to all

intuition. I have put the term "applicable" in quotes because the application in question is not an empirical application of concepts to intuitions—
the problem is that concepts and intuitions spring from faculties whose
functions are irreducibly different, so there is the possibility that intuitions *as such* might be incapable of being brought to the unity of consciousness under concepts. The problem of the Deduction, then, is to show the
a priori applicability of the categories to all intuition that can be given to
us—that is, to show that our sensible intuitions as such are capable of
being united under categories *as such.* The proof of the a priori applicability of categories to intuitions would then be what makes possible a
priori synthetic (propositional) judgments. (For example, if it has been
shown that the category of cause/effect applies a priori to everything that
can be given in our intuition, then it can be proved that "all alterations
take place in conformity with the law of the connection of cause and effect"—KrV B232.)

(It should also be noted that strong support for Henrich's position on
this point is to be found in Kant's redefinition of the concept of a judgment
in Section 19—KrV B141—2: "I find that a judgment is nothing but the
manner in which given cognitions are brought to the objective
unity of apperception." This formulation clearly implies that the question
of a priori synthetic judgments is not in the first place simply a question
of a priori synthetic propositions but rather a question of the a priori
relation of different cognitive faculties.)

This interpretation of the basis of the question of a priori synthetic
judgments gives us a way of seeing how that feature of transcendental
arguments could apply to arguments other than that of the first Critique.
The roots of theoretical knowledge are intellect and sensible intuition.
But the roots of practical knowledge, for example, are intellect and the
faculty of desire. So the problem of a priori synthesis for practice is
the problem of the a priori relation of reason to the faculty of desire
(that is, the "material" of practical knowledge would be will-determinations rather than intuitions). And the moral law would be an a priori

synthetic judgment not because it asserts a connection between concepts, but because it asserts an a priori connection between a rule of reason and the faculty of desire (it asserts a determination of the will by pure reason).

But this interpretation also allows us to make a connection between the two features of transcendental arguments: The a priori relation between the two roots of (for example) theoretical knowledge is a presupposition not only of a priori synthetic *judgments* but also of *experience* (and, in fact, of the theoretical viewpoint itself). In the chapter on the Principles in the first Critique, therefore, Kant argues that the principles—a priori synthetic judgments—are conditions of the possibility of experience precisely because they presuppose the same synthetic relation between faculties that experience itself presupposes.

So the two features are linked, and their common basis is the finitude of the human mind—that is, the fact that for us (according to Kant) knowledge always involves more than one root (KrV A50/B74; B135): The human intellect is discursive, which means that it functions through concepts. Concepts are unity-functions, and they presuppose a manifold to be unified. But intellect cannot itself supply that manifold—that must be given from elsewhere. For theoretical cognition the manifold is given by intuition, and without intuitions concepts are empty (KrV A51/B75). It will turn out that the situation is different with practical reason: Practical reason does always require a content (the "manifold of desires"— cf. 65), but in this case reason *is* capable of producing its object (a will-determination). Nevertheless, the will that reason determines is a faculty of desire that is conditioned by sensibility, and it therefore functions according to rules that are irreducibly distinct from those of reason. So there is a question of the a priori relation of faculties for practical reason as well as for theoretical reason.

The two features of transcendental arguments would then be simply different manifestations of the fact that our knowledge always involves different faculties; and rather than simply looking for an application of the two features to contexts other than the theoretical, it would be reasonable to look for further evidence of the importance of the interrelation of faculties in determining the questions that must be answered by a transcendental argument.

We can therefore frame a preliminary model of a transcendental argument as follows: A transcendental argument will be concerned with establishing the conditions of the possibility of a cognitive framework (but a framework determined not arbitrarily but by necessary laws). And since the ultimate principle that must be referred to in establishing the "conditions of the possibility of..." is the principle of the unity of apperception (which guarantees the unity of the viewpoint), the argument will be concerned not with just any conditions whatsoever, but rather precisely with the conditions of the possibility of a priori relationships between faculties (that is, relationships between the faculties *as such* that allow them to function together to establish a unitary framework)—namely, between those faculties whose functioning is constitutive for the framework in question.

In application to the second Critique this preliminary model would lead us to expect that the argument is concerned with the conditions of the possibility of a practical framework and that the specific questions to be answered will relate to the a priori relationships between reason and the faculty of desire. (As a matter of fact, the faculty of desire will turn out not to be monolithic—it is treated in the Analytic first as a faculty of rational causality and then as a sensibly conditioned rational faculty.)

. . .

This preliminary model postulates the general aims and procedures of a transcendental argument, but it does not specify particular structures or particular questions that must be answered. To a certain extent, of course, those questions can only be raised with respect to the particular framework being considered (and so some specific questions will emerge out of our discussion of the criteria of a successful account of the Analytic in Section 3). But I think there is also more that can be said—

simply on the basis of the finitude of human cognition—about the particular kinds of questions that a transcendental argument deals with (the
primary sources for this discussion are the section on the Discipline of
Pure Reason in its Dogmatic Employment, KrV A712/B740—A738/B760;
also Crawford; and Henrich, 1969).

From the side of reason, human finitude means that our thinking is
discursive—the sole functions of our intellect are functions associated
with producing unity in a manifold, and although intellect supplies the
unity-functions (or at least the ultimate ground for the unity-functions—
the categories), it does not supply the manifold to be united (which must
be given by sensibility). These facts have many implications for the
method of philosophical proof: In the first place, philosophical arguments
are restricted to the analysis and synthesis of *concepts* ("Philosophical
knowledge is the knowledge gained by reason from concepts"—KrV
A713/B741). (It is true that we also have available to us pure formal intuitions that supply a nonempirical manifold, but these are of use only in
mathematics—*ibid.*) But concepts are empty unless they stand in some
determinate relation to a sensibly given manifold. Philosophical proofs,
however, in transcendental philosophy, cannot depend upon any empirical
material, because the aim is to account for the possibility of there being
a determinate relation between given material and concepts—that is, the
aim is precisely to establish a framework, so the argument cannot depend
upon data that could be given only within that framework.

(This situation is what leads to the necessity for transcendental arguments being grounded on the possibility of a framework: No given data
can ground the argument, but since some factual given is necessary if
the argument is not to be pure speculation, the reality of the givenness
of data in general within the framework must be taken as the ground of
the argument, so that an argument establishing transcendental principles
has an almost circular quality, since a transcendental principle has the
"peculiar character that it makes possible the very experience that is its
own ground of proof, and that in this experience it must itself always be
presupposed"—KrV A737/B765.)

So what we can conclude so far from the discursive nature of the human intellect is that (1) philosophical arguments can involve only concept-manipulation (although factual givens must be appealed to to ground the argument), and (2) those concepts cannot be empirical concepts. Therefore philosophy deals with concepts, and with concepts that must be capable of being given entirely a priori.

But (3) a priori concepts can never be *defined* in the strict sense—that is, we can never be sure that they are given in their entirety:

> ...no concept given a priori, such as substance, cause, right, equity, etc., can, strictly speaking, be defined. For I can never be certain that the clear representation of a given concept, which as given may still be confused, has been completely effected, unless I know that it is adequate to its object. But since the concept of it may, as given, include many obscure representations, which we overlook in our analysis, although we are constantly making use of them in our application of the concept, the completeness of the analysis of my concept is always in doubt...
> (KrV A728/B756).

This difficulty is not just an accidental weakness of the human intellect—it is rooted in the nature of a discursive intellect as such: Any concept—even an a priori concept—if it is an objectively valid concept, refers to an object that reason does not itself produce (concepts as such require a content, and they do not produce their own content). So there is an inherent limitation in the method of philosophy that is imposed on it by the discursive nature of our intellect: Philosophical arguments can proceed only by concept-manipulation, and yet the concepts with which they deal can never be assumed to be completely given. That means that philosophy cannot begin with definitions and proceed analytically to the implications of those definitions.

The solution to this difficulty is not to abandon concept-analysis as a mode of philosophical argumentation but rather to develop a method of argumentation that in some way compensates for the difficulty. The sort of argument needed would be one that begins with a provisional "definition" (we could use Kant's term for the most general meaning of definition: Erklärung) and draws certain conclusions from it by analysis; but the argument would then have to somehow take into account other determinations of the concept that were not explicitly considered in the original definition and analysis (but which might nevertheless be essential, a priori determinations of the object), since the "special character" of the other determinations "might occasion variety in the rule" (20—this quotation is, of course, taken badly out of context, but I think, nevertheless, that Kant is referring here to precisely the problem we are considering).

This sort of argument would have the form of proving first that something must be the case in general and then, as an additional but necessary step, showing how it can be the case in the particular instance. For that reason we can refer to this structure as the "must/can" structure.[4]

This formulation was first developed to account for the argument-structure of the B-edition deduction of the first Critique. The most blatant problem in that argument is that the same point seems to be proved twice (in Sections 20 and 26). The "applicability" of the categories to objects of the senses seems to be proved twice by two different arguments. So a central question regarding that argument's structure is What do the two steps prove, and how do they relate to each other (e. g., are they separate proofs or do they together form a single proof)?

The must/can distinction, applied to that argument, would imply that the first step of the argument proves that sensible intuitions in general (i. e., in abstraction from the particular nature of *our* intuition) must be subject to the categories a priori (and the argument is analytic and depends upon—among other things— the principle of the a priori unity of apperception). But that proof abstracts from the particular character of our intuition, so although it shows that our intuitions *must* be subject to the categories, it does not show that they *can* be subject to the categories. So the second step has to consider the mode in which a manifold is given to us (space and time) and show, on that basis, that everything that can be given is capable of being brought to unity under the categories.[5]

So the argument first considers the nature of sensible intuition *in general* (or *as such*—both of these expressions are used as translations of Kant's term *überhaupt*), and the second step then takes into account our particular forms of intuition to show (on separate grounds) that the conditions that they impose on cognition are a priori compatible with the conditions of a finite consciousness in general. The whole two-step argument is therefore synthetic. It is not complete until the end of the second step. And in a sense even the first step is incomplete without the second step since the objective reality of the concept of a sensible intuition in general is proved only by the possibility of experience—that is, the proof that x is true for intuition in general does not guarantee that x is true for every intuition or even for any particular intuition until we have established the objective reality of the concept and the field of its application). And yet, the conclusion of the first step is not empty—it is available for other applications as long as the level of its generality is kept in mind (and, in fact, Kant appeals to the conclusion of this first step in the second Critique—54).

So the must/can structure would in general involve a progression from a more general concept to a more determined concept. The more general concept would abstract from certain determinations that are a priori determinations of the object and therefore essential to it, but that are not essential to the *thought* of the object (for example, a "sensible intuition in general" is certainly *thinkable*, but the only intuition whose reality we know—namely, our own intuition—is a priori subject to the forms of space and time, which are not included in the concept of sensible intuition in general. So it is always possible that those particular forms impose conditions on intuition that are incompatible with subsumption under categories). That concept could then be analyzed to show its necessary consequences. But then it would still be necessary to reinstate the determinations that were abstracted from and to show—in a separate step and on different grounds—that those determinations are in fact compatible with the consequences derived from the more general concept.

This form of argument would frequently give the appearance of being repetitive, since, if we failed to recognize that essential determinations were abstracted from in the first step and must be considered in the second step, the same conclusion would seem to be drawn twice (or more than twice, since it might turn out that still further determinations must be taken into account). Or, if the conclusion in the second step is not drawn in the same terms as in the first, the second step might appear to be not repetitious but redundant. (So, for example, in the Analytic of the second Critique Kant's stated aim is to prove that pure reason can be practical—i. e., can determine the will; and that conclusion seems to be reached even before the Deduction. So a major problem in interpreting the Analytic is to show why the argument requires the Deduction and Chapters 2 and 3. My suggestion for a solution to that problem is that in Chapter 1 the will's nature as a faculty of desire is abstracted from, so the argument proves that pure reason *must* determine the will—and in this case the proof is by a combination of analytic argument and appeal to fact—but it does not show how reason *can* determine the will, granted that the will is a faculty of desire.) Therefore, if we adopt this structure into our model of transcendental arguments, then in our examination of Kant's arguments we should take apparent repetitions or redundancies as clues to the possible presence of the must/can structure.

It should be noted that although individual steps of the must/can argument may be analytic, the structure is essentially synthetic. That can be demonstrated by reduction (since if the argument as a whole were analytic then the additional determinations considered in the second step would have been already contained in the concept as considered in the first step, which is contrary to hypothesis); but it can be shown more interestingly if we recall the causes that produced the need for this kind of argument in the first place: It was because the human intellect is discursive rather than intuitive that philosophical arguments could not rely wholly on analysis, since a discursive intellect can never supply completely defined concepts a priori (except with reference to pure intuition, which is of use to mathematics but not to philosophy).

That means that all of the features of transcendental arguments that we have developed here have a common ground—namely, the finitude of the human intellect and its consequent dependence upon sensibility: That is the reason for the concern with a priori synthesis (interpreted as a priori synthetic relationships between faculties); it is the reason for the dependence upon the possibility of a cognitive framework as ground of proof (since the proof must be grounded on some factual given but cannot depend upon empirical data); and it is the reason for the must/can structure of individual arguments.

So our working model of a transcendental argument is as follows: A transcendental argument is one that is concerned with establishing the conditions of the possibility of a cognitive framework (in the sense outlined above). The problems of possibility that it will deal with will be problems of the possibility of a priori relations between different human faculties (how they unite, in the sense of functioning together, a priori to produce a given cognitive framework). In addition, we can expect to find in the argument a must/can structure that first establishes a point with respect to a deliberately restricted concept and then, on different grounds, shows the compatibility of further determinations with the conclusions of the first step.

If we wanted to establish these features with certainty *before* using them to interpret the argument of the Analytic of the second Critique, we would have to either derive them "empirically" from an examination of several of Kant's arguments or else show, in a much more rigorous way than we did above in deriving them, that they are necessarily tied up with the conditions of the possibility of philosophical arguments in transcendental philosophy. Both of these approaches would carry us beyond the scope of our present enquiry, but as evidence in favor of this model we can adduce the following two points: (1) The model includes (in generalized form) the two most commonly accepted features of transcendental arguments; and (2) all three features have a common ground—the finitude of the human intellect—which is itself one of the most fundamental principles of transcendental philosophy. But the ultimate test of this model will be its ability to make sense of the argument of the Analytic of the second Critique.

3. CRITERIA OF A SUCCESSFUL ACCOUNT OF THE ARGUMENT-STRUCTURE OF THE ANALYTIC OF THE SECOND CRITIQUE

The central reference point for our argument here is the text of the Analytic of the second Critique: The success of the argument must be judged by its ability to make sense of the actual wording of the text. But that general criterion must clearly be specified further, since Kant's text is incredibly dense and it would be unrealistic to expect to be able to give an account of everything in it.

Fortunately there are certain prominent and notorious difficulties with the text that are generally recognized as standing in need of explanation. Moreover, it is my opinion that these difficulties have never yet been adequately resolved. To establish this latter claim would require an examination of all the literature regarding the second Critique—a task that is clearly beyond our scope. I have, however, tried to show that these difficulties are still very much with us by examining the attempts of Beck and of Silber to resolve them. These examinations are given in Appendixes A and B, respectively. I take it as having been shown there that there remain major problems of interpretation and here I will simply enumerate those problems and indicate what questions they raise.

The major difficulties that face any interpretation of the argument of the Analytic of the second Critique can be divided into two classes: There are difficulties involving the Analytic as a whole, and there are specific difficulties raised by the individual chapters. I will begin with the first class of difficulties.

The first question that any interpretation of the argument must answer is What is the purpose of the Analytic as a whole? Kant himself says in the Preface that his purpose is "merely to show that there is a pure practical reason" (3). Although that is sometimes taken as being the aim of the argument, it is clearly not a sufficient aim for the entire Analytic, since that goal is reached already in Section 7 of Chapter 1, which would leave nearly 75 pages without a purpose.

This problem is all the more serious because without a clear under-standing of the unifying goal of the Analytic we cannot understand why it contains the steps that it does and why they are arranged as they are. (Beck, for example, in order to make sense of the Analytic, is forced to completely rearrange the parts, even subdividing chapters—see Beck 69-70 and our Appendix A.) The problems this raises will become even clearer when we see the difficulties raised by the individual chapters; but in general it is not clear why the argument has, for example, three chapters and why they are given in that order. (And Kant's explanations of the divisions of the Analytic—which involve comparisons with the structure of the first Critique—give the appearance of being mere pedantic concern with architectonic.) What we need, then, in order to understand the structure of the argument as a whole, in addition to a principle of unity, is a principle of division of the argument.

Closely related to these difficulties is the question of why Kant insists that the Critique is a critique of practical reason *in general* (or *as such*—überhaupt) rather than of *pure* practical reason (cf. 3, 15—16). (And this problem is aggravated by the fact that every chapter heading and sub-heading in the Analytic refers to the pure practical reason.) This difficul-ty extends to our interpretation of the individual parts of the argument as well, since at each step there is room for disagreement about whether it is practical reason in general or pure practical reason that is being considered.

So any account of the Analytic needs to be able to show what its ulti-mate goal is and why it pursues its goal in the steps that it does. And such an account must be able to show why the Critique is concerned with practical reason in general.

The second class of difficulties contains three major problems, corre-sponding to the three chapters of the Analytic: One involves the deduction, one involves the categories, and one involves the incentives.

The problem of the deduction is that the one thing that seems most clearly in need of a deduction not only is not deduced but is used to deduce something else. This turn of events is both unexpected and difficult to account for. (Beck, for example, acknowledges that the moral law is not the demonstrandum of the deduction, and yet he still seems inclined to search for such a deduction—see Appendix A.[6]) We need to be able to show why there is no need for (or possibility of) a deduction of the moral law, and why, on the other hand, there must and can be a deduction of freedom (and we need to see *to what extent* there can be a deduction of freedom).

The problem of the categories is related to the confusion between pure practical reason and practical reason in general: Kant twice states in unambiguous terms that the categories are categories of practical reason in general (or as such). These claims would not in themselves be so problematic except for the fact that the earlier parts of Chapter 2 seem to have been concerned with establishing an object of *pure* practical reason, and in that case the categories seem superfluous and confusing. So any account of Chapter 2 needs to be able to explain why the categories are of practical reason in general and why they are important to the argument of the chapter (and of the Analytic as a whole).

The problem of the incentives is that Kant proves in Chapter 1 that the moral law needs no incentive in order to determine the will—it determines the will immediately (that is what it means to prove that there is a *pure* practical reason). But in that case Chapter 3 (whose title is "The Incentives of Pure Practical Reason") seems to be either superfluous or in contradiction with Chapter 1: If pure reason needs an incentive in order to determine the will, then it does not determine the will immediately; and if pure reason does determine the will immediately, there is no need for an incentive. So we need to be able to understand why there must be a moral incentive in spite of the fact that that incentive is not required by reason in order to determine the will.

These, then, are the major difficulties with the text whose explanation I propose as criteria of the success of any interpretation of the argument. But, in addition, there is one more criterion that I would like to propose, even though it is based on a distinction that is far from being generally recognized—in fact, the distinction is usually ignored, and especially so in discussions of the moral philosophy.

The distinction in question is between an argument of empirical psychology and an argument based on a priori grounds. It might seem that the two kinds of arguments would be easily distinguishable, but in fact I think there is a basis for their being confused that is grounded in the fundamental stance of transcendental philosophy itself: The assumption of the transcendental standpoint is compared by Kant to the Copernican revolution (KrV Bxvi f.) because it proposes that phenomena be explained by reference to the viewer and the constitution of his or her mind. And it is the emphasis on the "constitution of the mind" that is subject to misinterpretation, since the mind can be treated either as an object of empirical psychology or as an object of a priori knowledge.

Now there can be no doubt that transcendental philosophy considers the mind solely through a priori concepts, and, in fact, no empirical grounds at all can enter into arguments of transcendental philosophy:

> What has to be kept chiefly in view in the division of such a science [viz., transcendental philosophy] is that no concepts be allowed to enter that contain in themselves anything empirical, or, in other words, that it consist in knowledge wholly a priori (KrV A14/B28).

So transcendental arguments, unlike arguments of empirical psychology—and in spite of the fact that both kinds of arguments deal with "the constitution of the mind"—deal only with a priori concepts. This restriction applies to transcendental philosophy as such and therefore to practical as well as theoretical philosophy. And the application of this restriction to moral philosophy seems to have at first convinced Kant that, for that reason, moral philosophy could not be made a part of transcendental philosophy. In fact, the passage quoted above continues

Accordingly, although the highest principles and fundamental concepts of morality are a priori knowledge, they have no place in transcendental philosophy, because, although they do not lay at the foundations of their precepts the concepts of pleasure and pain, of the desires and inclinations, etc., all of which are of empirical origin, yet in the construction of a system of pure morality these empirical concepts must necessarily be brought into the concept of duty, as representing either a hindrance, which we have to overcome, or an allurement, which must not be made into a motive. Transcendental philosophy is therefore a philosophy of pure and merely speculative reason. All that is practical, so far as it contains incentives, relates to feelings, and these belong to the empirical sources of knowledge (KrV A14/B28-A15/B29).

This is the only case in my argument in which I will maintain that Kant must have changed his opinion (since that mode of explaining apparent contradictions in Kant's text is one that I think should, as a general principle, be avoided). But the reason Kant was able, after all, to include an analysis of the faculty of desire in the second Critique was by no means a change of mind about the admissibility of empirical components into transcendental philosophy. On the contrary, it was Kant's realization that these empirical concepts could be given Erklärungen making use only of "terms belonging to the pure understanding" (9n) that allowed him to apply the methods of transcendental argumentation to moral philosophy. He gives the necessary transcendental Erklärungen in a footnote to the Preface of the second Critique:

Life is the faculty of a being by which it acts according to the laws of the faculty of desire. The faculty of desire is the faculty such a being has of causing, through its representations, the reality of the objects of those representations. Pleasure is the representation of the agreement of an object or an action with the subjective conditions of life, i.e., with the faculty through which a representation causes the reality of its object (or the direction of the energies of a subject to such an action as will produce the object) (9n).

It is only the possibility of framing these Erklärungen that involve solely a priori concepts that allows us to carry out a critique of practical reason in general.[7] Correspondingly, the Critique is justified in dealing with the faculty of desire only through these concepts: Any other concepts will depend upon empirical determinations, and use of such concepts will transform the argument from one of transcendental philosophy to one of empirical psychology.

So the final criterion that I propose is that any interpretation of a transcendental argument must not reduce transcendental problems to problems of empirical psychology. With respect to the second Critique that means, in particular, that we will not be concerned with questions of the empirical application of the moral law to action—if Kant speaks of "applying" the moral law (as he does in the Typic), that will have to be interpreted to mean a priori "application," which involves analyzing human faculties according to their transcendental Erklärungen and showing how relations among them are possible a priori. (What is excluded by this criterion is, for example, interpretations that read the Typic as being concerned with supplying a "schema" for empirical application of the law in acting, or that read the chapter on the incentives as supplying a "motive power" for the moral law. Both Beck and Silber seem to frequently fall into this error—see Appendixes A and B.) If an interpretation cannot account for an argument except by reducing its concerns to questions of empirical psychology, then it cannot be counted a successful interpretation.

PART II
THE ARGUMENT OF
THE ANALYTIC

4. PRELIMINARY OUTLINE OF THE ARGUMENT OF THE ANALYTIC AS A WHOLE

In the preceding chapter I listed the most notable difficulties confronting any interpretation of the argument of the Analytic. In this chapter I will give a preliminary outline of my account of the argument of the Analytic in order to show the approach I intend to take in dealing with these difficulties.

The first difficulty was to give an account of the Analytic as a whole that would both show the unity of the argument and account for its division into the separate steps that it contains. My approach will be to argue that the unifying concern of the Analytic is to establish a peculiarly practical viewpoint distinct from the theoretical that includes both pure and empirically conditioned practical reason. We can deal with these two points separately, treating first the need for a practical viewpoint distinct from the theoretical and then the inclusion of both pure and sensibly conditioned willing (and it will turn out that in the process of dealing with these questions the difficulties concerning the separate chapters of the Analytic will also be dealt with).

A viewpoint in general is an organizational framework for unifying phenomena. If the viewpoint is to be objective, the unity must be based not upon arbitrary principles but upon necessary principles. This fact can be reformulated in two different but closely linked ways: (1) An objective viewpoint presupposes principles of necessary (and therefore a priori) unity and ultimately presupposes a highest principle of a priori unity to which everything in the framework must be subject. And (2) an objective framework presupposes *laws* (objectively valid principles) and ultimately a priori laws. Both of these presuppositions are important to the argument of the Analytic of the second Critique since Kant's way of establishing that there *must be* a practical viewpoint (Chapter 1) is by showing that there is a practical law, and since his way of showing that there *can be* such a viewpoint is by showing the a priori conditions of the possibility of uniting all sensibly conditioned principles with the moral

law a priori under the concept of freedom (i. e., showing that the moral
law is the "supreme condition" of all willing—cf. 31, 62, 86, 110).

The second point has to do with the inclusion of sensibly conditioned
willing in the practical viewpoint; but the first, and prior, point concerns
the problem of showing that there *must be* such a viewpoint at all. To
show that, we need to prove that there is at least one practical law that
must be recognized as objectively necessary (i. e., as being more than
a mere thought) and that that law is irreducibly distinct from from all
natural laws—that is, it must be shown that the laws depend ultimately
upon totally different *faculties*. (This point, which is crucial for the
proof of Chapter 1, turns out to provide the chief difficulty that must be
dealt with in Chapters 2 and 3, since the will is subject to two fundamentally distinct kinds of laws but must nevertheless be subject to the a
priori unity of a pure will.)

It is because the viewpoint is established by a *law* that Kant is able to
use the (legalistic-sounding) expression "realm" in this context. Kant
introduces this term in the third Critique:

> Concepts, so far as they are referred to objects apart from
> the question of whether knowledge of them is possible or not,
> have their field, which is determined simply by the relation
> in which their Object stands to our faculty of cognition in
> general. —That part of this field in which knowledge is possi-
> ble for us is a territory (*territorium*) for these concepts and
> the requisite cognitive faculty. The part of the territory over
> which they exercise legislative authority is the realm (*ditio*)
> of these concepts and their appropriate cognitive faculty (KU
> Introduction, Section II).

But the emphasis here on "lawful authority" should not mislead us into
ignoring the fact that what laws do is to establish necessary connections
among phenomena and thus make *knowledge* possible.

So according to our account the second Critique must first establish
that there *must be* a practical realm distinct from the theoretical, and
that is done by showing (in Chapter 1, Sections 1—7) that there is a
peculiarly practical law (the moral law). (This task is simply our
reformulation of Kant's stated aim of showing that there is a pure practical reason.) In order to show that the existence of a practical law presupposes a practical viewpoint Kant shows that the moral law presupposes freedom (Section 8) and that that, in turn, can only be rendered
intelligible if we presupposes a practical viewpoint that includes natural
phenomena under practical laws. (And this shows why the Deduction
contains a deduction not of the moral law but of freedom. It also shows
that what is deduced is not the *concept* of freedom simply, because that
cannot be deduced within a theoretical framework. What the deduction
does instead is to *shift* the framework by arguing for the necessity of a
practical framework. But even on those terms the deduction is not wholly
complete, because it does not show how such a framework is possible,
given the sensible nature of the will. That problem leads us into our
second point, namely, the need for a critique of practical reason as such.)

A viewpoint is a framework within which knowledge is possible. The
practical viewpoint is a framework within which knowledge of *what to do*
is possible. That is, practical knowledge always involves will-determinations: Any practical judgment, if it is to count as knowledge, must either
actually contain a will-determination or contain the grounds for a possible
will-determination (cf. Logic 94; Ethics 1—3). The will-determination in
the practical realm functions like intuition in the theoretical inasmuch
as it supplies evidence of the objective reality of the judgment. (For a
pure will a "logical"—i. e., pure rational—determination would at the
same time be a will-determination. But for a finite will rational determinations and will-determinations are irreducibly distinct: Logical
necessity is not the same as practical necessity.)

In thought we can abstract from the aspect in which finite will-determinations differ from the determinations of a pure will—that is, we can

abstract from their material aspect (the content of the practical knowledge); and that abstraction is actually necessary in order to establish
the practical law, since the moral law *excludes* all material from the
will's determining grounds. Nevertheless, the human will is not a pure
will (which exists for us only in thought) but rather a sensibly conditioned
will—sensible conditions are never entirely absent from willing, even
though they may be present only as opposition to pure moral will-determinations. So any argument concerning the will that totally abstracted
from the will's relation to a content and that considered the will only as
practical reason would not be able to claim objective reality for its
conclusions.

Another way of saying this is to point out that the practical framework
is not a framework for organizing *noumena*, it is a framework for
organizing *phenomena*. The material content of practical judgments—
including will-determinations and their accompanying feelings of pleasure
and pain—are themselves phenomena that could be viewed from a theoretical viewpoint as well. So the practical realm differs from the theoretical not because it includes different data but because the data (phenomena) are subject to different principles of unity. This is expressed by
Kant in the third Critique (again in terms of realms) as follows:

> Our entire faculty of cognition has two realms, that of natural
> concepts and that of the concept of freedom, for through both
> it prescribes laws a priori. In accordance with this distinc-
> tion, then, philosophy is divisible into theoretical and practi-
> cal. But the territory upon which its realm is established, and
> over which it *exercises* its legislative authority, is still always
> confined to the complex of the objects of all possible experi-
> ence, taken as no more than mere phenomena...(KU Introduc-
> tion, Section II).

So the practical viewpoint must be able to include sensible conditions
on willing, and that is why we need a Critique of practical reason *as
such*: If there is to be a unified practical viewpoint there cannot be sensible conditions that stand in *no relation whatsoever* to moral determining
grounds (which is the possibility raised by the discovery, in Chapter 1,

that there is a moral law that is irreducibly distinct from natural law).
That means that the practical viewpoint must be able to include within
its framework (and include them a priori) conditions imposed on willing
by its existence in the realm of nature and as subject to empirical determinations (according to laws of nature). But transcendental philosophy
cannot deal with those conditions through empirical concepts (since that
would reduce the level of argument to that of empirical psychology, which
presupposes a theoretical framework). Instead, we must make use of
Kant's transcendental Erklärungen: The will's sensible nature can be
dealt with only insofar as it can be brought under pure concepts.

What it means for the will to be sensibly conditioned is that the will
always has an object (which presupposes the functioning of practical
understanding in bringing a manifold of desires under the concept of the
good) and that that object can serve as determining ground for the will
only through its relation to the faculty of pleasure and pain. So Kant
deals with the problem of bringing the will's sensible nature into the
practical framework in two steps: First (Chapter 2) he abstracts from
the function of the faculty of pleasure and pain (the fact that the will is
always conditioned by pleasure) and treats the will's sensible nature
solely with respect to the fact that the will must have an object (and he
gives a transcendental Erklärung of "object" to correspond to this abstraction). But he is not concerned with *specifying* an object (or "providing the law with an object")—the question here is How can there be objects
at all in a practical realm? And that problem (as will generally be the
case in transcendental philosophy if our account is right) resolves quite
specifically into the problem of how two faculties can be brought to unity—
namely, pure practical reason (which provides the sole objective law for
the realm) and practical understanding (whose categories are categories
of a possible nature). (From this can be seen our solution to the difficulty
involving the fact that the categories of freedom are said to be categories
of practical reason in general: Categories of practical reason in general
are precisely what is required to bring a manifold of desires—considered

solely as objects of the will, not as pleasurable or painful—to unity under a pure will whose highest law is the moral law. In other words, the generality of the categories is not an anomaly but, rather, precisely what we need for the argument. *How* the categories perform their function is, it is true, a more difficult question, and we will have to deal with that in Section 6.)

But even after we show that the unity of the practical viewpoint is compatible with the will's having an object (that is, even after having dealt with the will's objective material content—cf. 75 and 16), we need to show that it is compatible with the *subjective* conditions imposed on the sensibly conditioned will by the faculty of pleasure and pain (that is, we need to deal with the will's subjective material content). That is done (in Chapter 3), once again, by the use of transcendental Erklärungen, this time of pleasure, pain, incentive, and interest. (And from this we can see why there needs to be a chapter on incentives: not in order to supply the moral law with motive power, but to show how the will's subjective sensible nature is compatible with the a priori unity of a practical framework whose law is the moral law. Kant's solution is to show that the moral law, in immediately determining the will, also stands in an a priori determining relationship to the faculty of pleasure and pain as a whole. So the moral law, in determining the subjective grounds of willing a priori, guarantees the subjective unity of the practical realm.)

This, then, is, in outline form, my account of the argument-structure of the Analytic. The account could be summed up briefly by saying that the Analytic is concerned with showing that there is an objective practical viewpoint (different from the theoretical viewpoint) within which the moral law is the supreme condition of all willing. To say that the moral law is the supreme condition of all willing is not to say that it is a condition of the possibility of all willing, since in that case immoral willing would have been proved to be impossible; rather, it is to say that the moral law is the sole law of practical reason and that it limits all sensibly conditioned willing a priori. But the moral law's being the supreme condition of all willing is itself a condition of the possibility of a practical viewpoint, since the unity of the viewpoint demands that there not be any sensible condition on willing that stands in no relation whatsoever to the moral law (which is the sole law of freedom).

We next need to use this outline to actually unravel the argument of the Analytic.

5. THE ARGUMENT OF CHAPTER 1

The main purpose of the first chapter of the Analytic, according to our account, is to show that there must be a practical viewpoint. That requires showing that natural phenomena must be viewed as subject to laws other than those of nature. So the establishing of a practical viewpoint amounts to establishing a different cognitive and existential framework for objects: Objects of a practical viewpoint are then no longer merely naturally determined phenomena that must be *given* in order to be real; instead, their reality is noumenally grounded and is revealed by the will's determination to produce them. The practical viewpoint is a product of the interaction of reason and the will rather than reason and intuition; practical forms are rules, and practical content is will-determinations.

The chapter achieves its purpose in a series of arguments that do not immediately seem to be concerned with establishing a practical viewpoint. Kant talks, instead, about proving "that there is a pure will" or "that pure reason can be practical" (e. g. , 15—16, 41—42). But I think this apparent discrepancy is due to the must/can structure of the argument, which gives the chapter the form of a set of "nested" arguments. The innermost core of this nest of arguments is the proof that pure reason is practical (Sections 1—7). This is a must-argument and is strictly analytic except for the introduction of the Fact of pure practical reason (it is because the argument is analytic that it can be put in the form of theorems and corollaries). But from this conclusion it follows (again analytically) that the will must be free (Theorem IV), and with this conclusion we have stepped beyond the bounds of the theoretical viewpoint. So the question of whether there *is* a pure will (which, on its first being posed, could be mistakenly interpreted as a question of theoretical knowledge—namely, whether in fact there is such an entity as a pure will) turns out to be a question of the need for an objective practical viewpoint distinct from the theoretical. That there must be such a viewpoint is established in the Deduction.

The Deduction, therefore, although it seems to be a separate step in the argument, is really required by and to an extent presupposed in the proof

of the theorems, since without the Deduction the proof of the theorems
would contain a conclusion that seems self-contradictory—namely, that
there really exists a cause that is unconditioned. This contradiction is not
given thematic consideration in the theorems, but it ultimately cannot be
avoided; and without the Deduction it would seem to invalidate the proofs
of the theorems.

This same nested structure appears on a larger scale in the Analytic as
a whole, since the argument for the objective reality of a practical realm
presupposes the unity of that realm, and the possibility of that unity is
established only in Chapters 2 and 3. In each case the argument proceeds
by first establishing what *must* be the case and then showing how that is
possible; and in each case the proof that something must be the case takes
place on a higher level of generality than the proof that it can be the case
—the "can"-proof involves taking into consideration particular conditions
that were left out of account in the "must"-proof. The Deduction, for example, takes into account the fact that the will as a faculty of desire is
subject to laws of nature, a problem that was held in abeyance in the
proofs of the theorems. The Deduction treats the relation of laws of nature to the will only in an abbreviated form, however, arguing simply that
there must be an intelligible order to which the natural order is subject.
The argument is, from the point of view of the theorems, a "can"-argu-
ment; but from the point of view of Chapters 2 and 3 it is a "must"-argu-
ment, and it requires supplementation by an explanation of how that realm
is possible (an explanation which those latter two chapters provide).

So in spite of the fact that Kant presents the aim of Chapter 1 as being
simply to prove that the will can be free, I think we will see that the proof
actually bursts the bounds of experience and renders necessary a redefinition of objective reality for practice—a redefinition that is not confined
to the interrelation of concepts and intuitions but must rather involve
"dynamical laws" of action (cf. 42).

Our account of the theorems will therefore present them as arguing for
the existence of a realm of freedom by adducing a law of that realm that

cannot be reduced to natural lawfulness: First it must be shown what kind
of law would have to be adduced to establish such a realm (it must be
shown that such a law and only such a law would establish such a realm);
second, the factual existence of that very law must be adduced; and
finally, the reality of that realm can be concluded.

But before the theorems can be proved, the concept of law must be
clarified and distinguished from other kinds of practical rules, especially
maxims (I am taking Kant's term "rule" to be the generic term that includes maxims and laws as species, like, for example, the term "representation," which is a generic term including concepts, intuitions, etc.
This interpretation is in contrast to Beck's interpretation—cf. Beck,
1966, 79—which would restrict the term so that rules would be distinguished from both maxims and laws.)

The Erklärung and its Remark

The Analytic begins not with a definition but with a clarification of the
terms "law" and "maxim." A full definition of these terms would be possible only after the completion of the Analytic. Instead of defining them,
Kant simply points to the distinguishing feature of the two that is necessary for the theorems that follow: Laws are objective and valid for everyone, maxims are valid only for a particular subject (19). So the question
of the existence of a realm of freedom (the question of the determination
of the will by pure reason) can be decided by determining whether or not
there are practical laws. ("Assuming that pure reason can contain a practical ground sufficient to determine the will, then there are practical
laws; otherwise all practical principles are mere maxims"—*ibid.*, first
sentence of the Remark.)

This opening Erklärung is not only not a definition in the strict sense
(for example, since it does not allow of construction like mathematical
definitions, we are not assured ahead of time of the existence of the object
defined—indeed, that is the point of the theorems)—it is also not obvious
that it works as a clarification. This is indicated by the general confusion
surrounding it. Beck, for example—in contrast to Kant's own division—

argues that since some maxims have a lawful form and others do not, laws must, strictly speaking, be a subclass of maxims (" 'maxim' is broader than 'law' and, in fact, includes 'law' as one of its species"— Beck, 1966, 81).

In the Remark to the Erklärung Kant seems to confuse matters further rather than clearing things up: First he points out that a "practical rule is always a product of reason" (20), and that presumably means both maxims and laws. Then he introduces the term "imperative," asserting that a rule "for a being whose reason is not the sole determinant of the will" (*ibid.*) appears as necessitation, and he says that imperatives must therefore be clearly distinguished from maxims along just those lines (so that maxims would seem *not* to be products of reason—and yet, insofar as they are rules, it would seem that they *must* be products of reason in some sense).

The difficulties surrounding the Erklärung and its Remark show, I think, that we do not need only to understand the *distinction* between maxims and laws (which is actually fairly straightforward: The former are subjectively valid principles while the latter are objectively valid), but, even more, we need to know what a maxim *is* and how it *functions* as a maxim as well as what a law is and how it functions as a law.

This enquiry is all the more important in light of the fact that the moral law, when it is finally introduced, turns out to be a *law* for *maxims* ("Always act in such a way that the maxim of your will could at the same time hold as a universal law")—a law that seems to command that laws *become* maxims (however we might understand that). I think this can only be understood if we interpret the distinction between maxims and laws not as a distinction of different *kinds* of principles (e. g. , universalizable and nonuniversalizable) but rather as a distinction that concerns the way principles *function* with respect to the will. And I think that that sort of interpretation will better allow us to see Chapter 1 as establishing a realm of freedom over the territory of natural phenomena.

I have relegated the detailed examination of this question to an Appendix (Appendix D: Maxims and Laws). Here I shall simply summarize the results of that examination.

The human will is a complex faculty involving functions that are separable in thought even thoug not in fact. Kant uses the terms Wille and Willkür to distinguish the two most basic functions of the will (this distinction is formally introduced and adhered to only in the later moral writings, e.g. , the *Metaphysics of Morals* and the *Religion within the Limits of Reason Alone*; in the second Critique the word Willkür rarely occurs, and the word Wille seems to be used to mean the will as a whole, having both functions). They correspond to the distinction between the will viewed in relation to its determining grounds (which are always rules and therefore products of the rational faculty) and the will viewed in relation to its actions (which are always events in the natural realm and therefore stand in relation to sensibility). From either viewpoint the will is both a faculty of desire (appetitive faculty) and rational. But when we speak of will as Wille (in the strict sense) we are not considering its relation to the natural realm (so, for example, we could not say that it is free or even that is acts)—rather, we are considering it as pure *spontaneity*; whereas, when we speak of will as Willkür we are considering it as a particular kind of *natural* causality, namely, causality by reason (whether pure or not).

These two functions of will are both rule-governed, but they are essentially distinct and irreducible. Both Wille and Willkür operate according to principles (and the principles might be the same in both cases—"same" in the sense of having the same *verbal* expression) , but their principles function in fundamentally different ways.

Principles of *Wille* as such are always *laws*, principles of *Willkür* are *maxims*; and the functions of laws and maxims are distinct: To be a *maxim* a principle must be tied up with the acting subject's own subjective conditions of acting (which are necessarily sensible conditions and therefore dependent upon laws of nature)—it must be *adopted* as a maxim. To be a *law* a principle must *exclude* all sensible conditions, and it functions as a law precisely insofar as it is recognized as representing determining grounds radically different from sensible, naturally conditioned determining grounds.

So a maxim can never simply *become* a law, nor can a law simply become a maxim, because they represent determinations under essentially different realms (the realms of nature and of "supersensible nature"— 43). A universalizable maxim willed morally does not cease to be an expression of causality under the laws of nature. What the moral law expresses is the necessary subordination of natural causality to supersensible determining grounds: To be willed morally the principle expressed in the maxim must be willed as *both* maxim (and therefore as an expression of natural lawfulness) *and* law (and therefore as an expression of pure rational lawfulness); and the former must be willed as subordinate to the latter (that is, the maxim as natural causality must be chosen *for the sake of* its pure lawful form).

This account of the distinction between laws and maxims and the sense in which they can be united must not be understood only on the level of "practical epistemology." What it means to say that maxims must be willed as subordinate to laws—granted that the laws can never be laws of nature but only of a supersensible nature—is that, in acting, the natural world as a field of action, with all its causes and effects, must be represented as having its ground in a noumenal order whose highest law is the moral law. So the practical Critique reopens the question of the ontological status of objects of experience and reconfirms the answer supplied in the first Critique (namely, that those objects are appearances of noumena which cannot themselves appear but still must be presupposed as necessary thoughts), but with the further stipulation that—for the purposes of action—the noumenal grounding of phenomena is of the first importance. In the realm of action noumena are not merely necessary thoughts: They supply the highest ground of determination of the will. And it is this difference that determines the course of the argument of the Analytic, since the objects of experience must be viewed (for the purposes of action) both as phenomena—in exactly the same sense as in the first Critique—and as effects of a noumenal causality; and we need to show how objects *can* be viewed that way.

These latter considerations show more fully what was suggested above —namely, that the full understanding of laws and maxims requires the completion of the entire Analytic, since we need to see how maxims as subject to natural laws (which they always are since they always have not merely a lawful form but also a material content as the effect for the sake of which the object is willed) can be subordinated to laws of freedom.

But for the moment we have accomplished what was needed, namely, to indicate how from the very outset the distinction between laws and maxims raises the ontological question of the possible existence of a realm of freedom and a practical viewpoint. (For the more detailed examination of this question, see Appendix D: Maxims and Laws.) That being done, we can proceed to the next tasks, which are to show what must be the nature of a law that could establish a realm of freedom (KpV Sections 2—4), to adduce the factual reality of such a law (KpV Sections 5—7), and finally to conclude that the will must be free (Section 8) and that there must be a realm of freedom (the Deduction).

Sections 2—4

Theorem I

Sections 2—4 are concerned with showing what sort of principle would have to be adduced to establish the reality of a practical realm distinct from the realm of nature (the ultimate aim being to then show that *there is* such a principle and therefore *there is* such a realm). Theorem I takes the first step by starting with an examination of principles that presuppose an object (material) as determining ground. It should be noted at the outset that Kant does not introduce the formal/material distinction in the first place as a distinction of *kinds* of practical principles but rather as a distinction of how principles *function* in determining the will. This gives support to our thesis that what is at stake in the argument is not the

relationship between propositional features of practical principles (subjects and predicates; or the quantity of the judgement) but rather the relationship between faculties of the will: To find a principle that can establish a practical realm means to find a law, and a law is not just a particular kind of principle but rather a principle that does in fact function in a
particular way in determining the will. When Kant does speak of material
principles and formal principles it must be kept in mind that the distinction refers to the way the principle is functioning in willing and not to
features that can be read off from the principle stated as a proposition.

The first theorem, then, proves two things: (1) that all principles that
presuppose an object of the faculty of desire as determining ground of the
will are empirical and (2) that therefore they cannot serve as (practical)
laws.

The proof of (1) is as follows: A principle that presupposes the existence
of an object as the determining ground of the will—a material principle—
has a determinate relation to a subject's will only insofar as the object of
the principle is desired by the subject. For an object to be desired by a
subject it must be represented by the subject as standing in a determinate
relation to the subject's own sensibility (pleasure or pain). But a determinate relation to sensibility can only be known empirically. Therefore
any principle that presupposes such a determinate relation of an object
to the subject's sensibility (as a condition of the principle's possibility)
is an empirical principle.

The proof of (2) follows immediately: Material principles depend upon
the receptivity of the subject, which can only be known empirically and is
therefore not necessarily the same for all subjects. So the principles are
not objectively but only subjectively valid and therefore cannot serve as
(practical) laws. (They cannot represent a necessary connection between
cause and effect on grounds of intellect alone but must rather import
sensible conditions to produce necessitation. That is the distinguishing
feature of maxims as opposed to laws - cf. Appendix D: Maxims and
Laws.)

Theorem II

The proof of Theorem I leads, without any Remark, immediately into Theorem II, which asserts that all material principles belong under the general principle of self-love or one's own happiness. (The relevance of this theorem will become clearer when we consider the Remarks appended to it.) The proof of this theorem follows simply from the analysis of material principles outlined in the preceding theorem together with the definition of happiness: All material practical principles presuppose the represented existence of an object as determining ground of the will, and the existence of an object can be represented as determining for a will only insofar as the object is represented as given to sensibility and given as agreeable. So what is really at stake in material principles is not the state of an *object* but rather the state of the *subject* as agreeable or disagreeable. But happiness is simply the general term for the subject's consciousness of agreeableness throughout an entire life, so any principle that refers to agreeableness as determining ground a fortiori refers to happiness as the general term under which agreeableness falls.

The Corollary reasserts the essential sameness of all material principles and points out that they are all grounded in sensibility (the "lower faculty of desire") so that unless there are pure formal laws of the will there exists no pure practical reason (the "higher faculty of desire").

The second theorem is followed by two Remarks, which are important for our interpretation of the argument. The first Remark points out, what will become absolutely crucial in Chapter 3, namely, that all will-determinations under the concept of self-love or happiness can differ from one another only in degree, no matter what may be the source of the represented happiness. The reason for that is that to the extent that different determining grounds all depend upon represented pleasure or displeasure they are all *qualitatively* the same (they are affections of the same "life-force"), so they can differ only in respect to the formal conditions of inner sense—that is, they can only differ with respect to intensity ("how

much") and extension ("how long" - cf. 23). This is completely in keeping with the Axioms of Intuition and Anticipations of Perception in the first
Critique (KrV A162/B202—A176/B218), and its real importance at this
stage in the argument is that it points to the fact (taken up immediately in
the second Remark) that material principles are principles that refer to
the will as *pathological*—that is, as subject only to laws of nature and
therefore viewed from a theoretical viewpoint.

The second Remark makes that point explicitly, and underlines it by
closing with the statement that

> This Remark may appear at first blush to be mere hair-splitting;
> actually it defines the most important distinction that can be con-
> sidered in practical investigations (26).

This "most important distinction" is, more precisely, the distinction
between theoretical necessity and practical necessity (which, seen from
the practical viewpoint, becomes the distinction between subjective necessity and objective necessity). The necessity expressed by a material principle is not illusory or contingent: From the theoretical point of view a
material principle is a necessary principle, since such a principle simply
expresses a connection of cause and effect according to laws of nature;
but it is necessary only for a given subject, since a different subject, although determined by the same causal law, would be influenced by different conditions. The one material principle that holds necessarily for *all*
subjects is the principle of self-love. But the necessity of the principle of
self-love does not derive from natural necessity but rather from the fact
that it is an analytic principle; and it is therefore empty of particular content: "To be happy is necessarily the desire of every rational but finite
being and thus it is an unavoidable determining ground of its faculty of
desire" (25; this is true because of the definition of a finite being as a
"being of needs" - *ibid.*). But the principle of happiness "is merely the
general name for subjective grounds of determination and determines
nothing specific concerning what is to be done in a given practical problem" (*ibid.*). The conclusion from all this is

Thus a *subjectively necessary* law (as a law of nature) is *objectively* a very *contingent* practical principle that can and must be very different in different subjects (25).

The significance of this for our interpretation is clear: Kant is arguing that all material principles without exception are principles for a will *in a realm of natural laws* and that, therefore, if there is a truly practical realm there must also be truly practical laws—that is, laws that determine the will by virtue of their *form* and not their content and which are therefore objectively valid in a *practical* sense (i. e., valid for all acting subjects as such rather than for a given acting subject as a natural object). This is the "most important distinction" because it points to a realm of freedom.

So the second theorem, although it might at first seem to be only a side-issue (since it is not obvious that we need to prove that all material principles fall under the principle of self-love in order to prove that only a pure formal principle can supply a practical law), turns out to be important to the thread of the argument since it establishes the distinction between material principles as pathological principles falling within a realm of nature and formal principles (if they exist) as nonpathological and therefore outside the realm of nature. It thus establishes that what is at stake is not just the will's recognition of this law or that but rather the will's existence as merely pathological or as also nonpathological.

Theorem III

The Remarks to Theorem II have carried us ahead of the actual argument of the theorems. One further step needs to be made formally (although it was implied in the Remarks): Theorem III proves simply that if there are to be laws that a subject will recognize as valid both objectively and subjectively ("if a rational being can think its maxims as practical universal laws" 27—8) then those laws must determine the will by virtue of their form rather than their content. The proof is simple: (1) It relies on Theorem I as having proved that a material principle cannot be a law; and (2) it introduces the further premise that besides the content of a principle there is nothing but the form. From these two premises it follows that

a rational being either cannot think of *his* subjective-practical
principles (maxims) at the same time as universal laws, or he
must suppose that their mere form, through which *they are fitted
for being universal laws*, is alone that which makes them a practical
law" (27).

(I have inserted the *zugleich*, which Beck omitted.)

The conclusion of this theorem could be expressed in slightly different

terms as follows: *Either* there are no practical laws distinct from natural

laws, in which case all practical principles are only maxims—that is, al-

though they may be universalizable rules of reason, they are related to the

faculty of desire only under contingent subjective conditions and so are

subject to no lawful necessity but that of nature—*or* the faculty of desire

is also determinable not only pathologically according to laws of nature

but also according to other laws by the mere lawful form of its maxims.

This reformulation of the theorem is, of course, designed to emphasize

that what is at stake is the existence of a realm of supersensible nature.

We also need to emphasize again the fact that the reality of practical

laws is seen as a problem involving not just propositional forms but voli-

tional functions. This is indicated by Kant's (rather surprising) emphasis

in the passage quoted above: The emphasis on "his" is intended, I think,

to indicate that it is not "a maxim in general" (e.g., "not to lie") that is

in question but a particular subject's maxim functioning in willing. There

is no doubt that a subject can follow the maxim of not lying (which is also

capable of being willed as a universal law); what *is* in doubt is whether a

particular subject can will *his* maxim of not lying (which must always have

been adopted into his own subjectivity and might not have been adopted

solely because of its lawful form) as *at the same time* a universal law, or

whether, in order to do so, he would have to eliminate from his willing of

the maxim precisely that factor that was responsible for his having adopt-

ed it in the first place (e.g., the prospect of happiness in an afterlife).

These points need to be emphasized, I think, because it is just such

points that mark the distinctive features of a transcendental argument: On

the one hand, as Kant's emphasis in this passage indicates, what is at

stake is not principles considered in abstraction from the willing subject
but rather the constitution of the will itself and its limitations (in particular, what is at stake is whether pure practical reason can determine the
faculty of desire). And, on the other hand, if it *can* be proved that the will
is in fact determinable by the mere form of a principle, that would mean
that the will is not subject only to pathological laws, which in turn would
point to the will's existence in an objective realm other than the realm of
nature. So the problem is framed from the start in terms of the interrelation of faculties of the will and their reference to an objective realm.

The Remark to the third theorem, in explicating what it means for a
maxim to be able to be willed as universal law, reemphasizes that practical laws, if they exist, must be laws for a realm that conforms to the requirements of a nature in general—that is, they must be conducive to a
systematic unity. The argument is, I think, that immoral maxims are all
instances of one or another particular kind of self-love (e. g. , avarice, in
the case of the maxim of increasing my own property by any safe means).
A universe governed by self-love under laws of avarice is perfectly con-
ceivable, but such laws could not produce a *practical* systematic unity:
Such laws could indeed serve as laws of a system of *sensible* nature, in
which case the unity they expressed would be the unity of a system of
natural objects governed by laws external to themselves. But that kind of
unity is, from the point of view of an acting subject, disharmony, since it
is not homogeneous with the purposeful activity of the subject. Thus Kant
can argue

> Empirical grounds of determination [i. e. , pathological determination]
> are not fit for any universal external legislation, and they are just as
> little suited to an internal, for each man makes his own subject,
> another, however, another subject, the foundation of his inclination,
> and in each person it is now one and now another that has preponder-
> ance. To discover a law that would govern them all under this condi-
> tion by bringing them into unison is absolutely impossible (29).

What is impossible is not systematic unity under pathological laws of
willing (nature presents precisely such a system) but rather such a unity
that at the same time accords with the purposiveness of wills. So, again,

what is at stake is a practical realm: a systematic unity under nonpathological laws.

Sections 5—7

The Problems

Kant has proved that either there are no practical laws (and therefore no
practical realm distinct from the realm of nature) or else the will must be
determinable by the mere lawful form of maxims. His next task is to establish that the will *is* so determinable.

The first step is to show that the determination of the will by the form of
maxims presupposes transcendental freedom (i.e., the will's subjection to
laws other than those of sensible nature) and conversely, that the reality
of transcendental freedom presupposes the will's determinability by the
mere lawful form of its maxims. The former is proved in Problem I by
arguing that if the will is determinable by the mere lawful form of its
maxims, since the form of a law is a representation of reason and not an
appearance, therefore the will is determinable by something that is not an
appearance. But to be subject solely to laws of nature means to be determinable only by appearances, so the will is not subject only to the laws of
nature but is, rather, transcendentally free. The converse is proved by
arguing that, granted that the will is determinable by laws, if the will is
free it is independent of all empirical conditions. But since the material of
the practical law must always be empirical, and since besides the content
of the law there is only the form, therefore a free will must be determinable by the mere form of a practical law.

In the Remark Kant points out that freedom of the will and its determinability by the mere form of a law are reciprocal concepts, so that if we
are given one we can always prove the other. The only question, then, is
whether we know either the reality of freedom or the determinability of the
will by the mere lawful form of its maxims. Kant's answer is that we can
never know the will to be free: We could never infer that from experience
(since experience must always be a thoroughgoing causal chain); but

neither could we derive the reality of freedom from mere concepts, since in that case the most we could prove would be that the will cannot *think* itself as determined by external causes when it is willing - we could never prove from concepts alone that the will really *is* free.

But we can, Kant argues, demonstrate that the will is determinable by the mere lawful form of its maxims. That demonstration really amounts to simply pointing to our awareness of moral obligation: The real demonstration that the will is determinable by the mere lawful form of maxims is to be found in our awareness that our own wills can be determined to action by the knowledge that an action is morally right and not solely by (and even in opposition to) consideration of our own interest. So Kant's demonstration is really his example: the man who is faced with the choice between death and the making of a false deposition against an honorable person. Insofar as we place ourselves in imagination in the position of that man and are aware of the force exerted on our own will by the thought of the rightness of the action, we become aware of the reality of moral obligation.

It is of prime importance to realize that the example by no means requires that we have the moral strength to actually perform the right action under those circumstances: Kant need not prove that people (or even one person) do actually act morally, but only that the will is determinable by nonpathological causes. The proof of that is not experience. What we have instead in the example is a preexperiential awareness through a feeling (respect) of our will being determined by a nonpathological cause. If the example required the actual performance of the action, then we could experience our will-determination in the strict sense, but in that case there would also always be present the moral satisfaction of the subject (in addition to whatever other advantages might be associated with the action), and that would be theoretically indistinguishable from a pathological motivation. So experience could never confirm determination of the will by pure reason alone. (This is the *subreption vitiones* that Kant refers to from time to time.)

This example raises real problems, since we need to see in detail, on
the one hand, how Kant avoids interpreting his example as *experience*—as
a fact in the sensible realm (in which case either he cannot demonstrate
the reality of a *pure* formal will-determination or he must contradict the
results of the first Critique), and, on the other hand, how he avoids eliminating both the *factual* quality of the demonstration and the relation of obligation to a real action in the natural world. For further consideration of
these questions see Appendix C: The Fact of Pure Practical Reason. For
now we need only emphasize those aspects of the demonstration that are
important for our interpretation of the argument as transcendental argument. For that purpose there are two major points to be made (to be developed in the next section): (1) that moral obligation appears as a *fact*,
and (2) that this Fact is *synthetic* because it asserts a necessary connection between a sensible determination and a rational determining ground.

The Fundamental Law

The law, when it is finally introduced formally, is

So act that the maxim of your will could always hold (gelten)
at the same time as a principle establishing universal law (30).

have already argued (cf. above and Appendix D) that the law asserts a
necessary relationship between irreducibly different faculties and their
determination: By commanding that maxims be able to be willed as at the
same time laws, the moral law is commanding a synthetic relationship between an intellectual determination (a law) and a sensible determination
(a maxim), it being understood that maxims never cease being subject also
to laws of sensible nature. Kant makes this point quite clearly in the Remark following the law and also in the Corollary and its Remark.

First he points out that the law is synthetic, and he connects this with the
fact that the law commands without "borrowing anything from experience or
any external will" (31). I take it that Kant is still making use of the meaning of practical analyticity that he outlined in the *Groundwork* (GMM 417,
20n)—namely, that a practical proposition is analytic if it presupposes
prior will-determination—and that that is what he means by "any external

will." That means that the law is synthetic, and the will-determination it asserts (commands) is not derived from some prior will-determination (and therefore not from the faculty of desire, which can originate will-determinations only as sensibly determined) but rather from reason: The law "only applies to the *subjective* form of principles [their function as principles of Willkür] and yet is a ground of determination by virtue of the objective form of law in general [principles functioning as laws of reason]" (31).

Secondly, Kant claims that the law is a *fact*. By referring to the law as a fact Kant can only mean, I think, that we really do (and must) recognize the law as binding—that is, that in thinking obligation as our own we are aware of actually being bound to a particular way of acting: We are aware of an actual will-determination. This awareness is not mere thought or subjective imagining. By virtue of its being an awareness of a determination of our causality (which has a necessary reference to experience, not as theoretical object but as practical object) it is objective. And yet the awareness is not experience: It is not given through intuition and so is not a function of our receptivity but rather of our spontaneity. In order to incorporate it into our experience we would have to treat the awareness as intuitional, which would mean treating it as representing our own agency as though it were a given phenomenon. That can be done, and in fact we frequently (if not usually) do think of our causality in that way—as being just another causal event in the realm of phenomena. (This is what Kant calls the process of subreption: Our own activity is represented—mistakenly—as a passivity.) But (or so I think Kant would argue) the awareness of moral obligation does not present itself to us in that way. In its fundamental presentation the awareness of moral obligation is not an experience but rather is recognized as a priori objective and factual. For further discussion of the Fact see Appendix C: The Fact of Pure Practical Reason.

The argument of Section 7 must, I think, be understood as a *demonstration*, in the sense of a pointing to or presentation of a thing whose objective reality needs no further proof. This is the sense in which Kant uses the term "demonstration" in the third *Critique*:"... if, as in anatomy, demonstration is understood in the sense merely of presentation [Darstellung] ..." (KU Section 57). (This is, of course, different from the strict meaning of "demonstration" given in the first Critique—KrV A734/B762 ff.) What is demonstrated is the moral law as determinative for our will; and it is demonstrated simply by exhibiting the actual will-determination. Whatever we may think of this demonstration (and I find it compelling), I think there can be no doubt that Kant considers it to be the exhibition of something that, once pointed out, is self-evident. His statements in the Deduction indicate that clearly: "the moral law is given as an apodictically certain fact, as it were, of pure reason, a fact of which we are a priori conscious..." (47).

We must keep in mind, however, that demonstrating the law as Fact is not the same as showing *how* the law can be the supreme condition of maxims, objects, and incentives—that is, it does not show how a practical viewpoint is possible within which such a fact could make sense. To exhibit the law as Fact is simply to show *that* it does determine our will, without rendering that determination intelligible or showing how it is possible. But to establish the moral law as supreme condition of all willing requires more than a presentation of facts—it requires an examination of the separate conditions imposed on willing by its finite character. That means examining the rational conditions of willing (for maxims), the conceptual conditions of willing (for objects), and the sensible conditions of willing (for incentives) to show that they are all compatible a priori with a practical framework. (The first is supplied by the argument of Chapter 1, the second by Chapter 2, and the third by Chapter 3.)

Section 8

It has been shown what sort of law must determine the will if the will is really to be able to be viewed as free, and it has been shown that such a law does in fact determine the will. Theorem IV draws the conclusion: The will must be free. (This should be compared with Silber's account of the argument in the theorems, according to which "Theorem IV is presupposed in the demonstration of Theorem III"—Silber, 1959b, 91 n20. That would be correct if what was being established were the necessity of the *thought* of autonomy for the *thought* of moral laws. But in fact, I think, what is being proved in the theorem is the objective reality of the positive concept of freedom.)

Theorem IV, then, contains two points: (1) "The autonomy of the will is the sole principle of all moral laws and the duties conforming to them" and (2) "heteronomy of Willkür ... not only does not establish any obligation but is opposed to the principle of duty and to the morality of the will."

The first point is proved by the same argument that was given in Problem I (Section 5): Since we now know that the will is determinable by the moral law, we know that the will is determinable by the mere lawful form of maxims; we therefore know the will to be determinable by a nonempirical, nonpathological law—i.e., we know the will to be free (autonomous).

The second point is proved as follows: Heteronomy would mean that the material of the will was contained in the will's principle as a condition of the principle's possibility as determinative for the will. In that case the principle would have the force of natural necessitation but not of practical necessitation (obligation); and, in fact, such a principle would depend upon a determining ground that must be excluded if the will is to be morally determined, so it is actually opposed to principles of duty.

The Remarks to this theorem focus primarily on underlining the distinction between the principle of happiness and the moral principle, which is not immediately relevant to our point. But we should notice that the second sentence of the first Remark asserts (what will be developed in the Deduction) that "the law of the pure will that is free places that will in a sphere entirely different from the empirical" (34). Even though nothing further seems to be made of this point here, I think it is in fact important to the train of argument of both Remarks—that is, I think the underlying argument against all varieties of happiness-morality is that they reduce willing to purely empirical phenomena and render it subject solely to natural necessitation by relegating it to the theoretical framework.

The point at which Kant's argument has arrived is that the will *must be* free. The proof has been entirely analytic except for the introduction of the moral Fact, and so it is apodictically certain. Yet, with the proof of Theorem IV, we have succeeded in establishing more than we can comprehend: The proof's certainty is gained at a loss of intelligibility. We now know that the will must be free, but we do not understand how that is possible. To the extent that the will's freedom can be made intelligible it is by showing the will to be a member of a realm of freedom. That is the task of the Deduction, to which we now turn.

The Deduction

Before we examine the text of the Deduction I will outline the approach I propose, making especial use of the model of transcendental arguments proposed in Chapter 2 and keeping in mind the criteria of a successful interpretation from Chapter 3.

As we saw in Chapter 3, the primary difficulty to be dealt with in Chapter 1 of the Critique is the fact that Kant denies the need for or possibility of a deduction of the moral law and gives instead (some sort of) a deduction of freedom:

> Instead of this vainly sought deduction of the moral principle something entirely different and unexpected appears: The moral principle itself serves as a principle of the deduction of an inscrutable faculty ... the faculty of freedom ... The moral law is a law of the possibility of a supersensuous nature ... (47).

But this passage, besides clearly stating that the moral law is not the demonstrandum of the argument, also suggests the way in which the deduction *should* be read: The deduction of freedom involves not just showing that freedom is a property of the will but establishing a *realm* of freedom (a "supersensuous nature").

The interpretation I propose for why the deduction should be concerned with these things is as follows: A transcendental argument requires an objective framework whose factual reality is certain. Theoretical reason can depend upon the undeniable reality of experience to guarantee its framework, but practical philosophy cannot assume such a framework at the outset. Instead, practical philosophy must first *establish* its framework. The process of establishing the practical framework, as exhibited in the deduction, can itself be seen as having the steps of a must/can argument: The Fact of the moral law's immediate determination of the will, taken together with Theorems I—IV, proves apodictically that the will *must* be free. But since free causality is a theoretically incomprehensible concept, we do not yet see how the will *can* be free. So the deduction argues that the will can be free only if viewed from a practical viewpoint distinct from the theoretical viewpoint. Therefore the deduction shows that there must be an objectively valid practical viewpoint.

This schematic account of the deduction, however, obscures the fact that there are important senses in which the deduction is incomplete. If we look at the deduction from the *theoretical* viewpoint, it offers a perfectly good must-step (assuming that we are willing to admit the Fact, even though it is not an experienced fact). But what the must-step establishes is that the will must be free, and for that conclusion no can-step is possible in the theoretical framework (since it would require showing "how the logical relation of ground and consequence could be synthetically used with another kind of intuition than the sensuous, i.e., how a *causa noumenon* is possible"—49). It is this impossibility that makes possible and requires the change of framework from theoretical to practical:

> Reason uses this concept only for a practical purpose, transferring the determining ground of the will to the intelligible order of things, and at the same time readily confessing that it does not understand how the concept of cause can determine knowledge of these things (49).

But even from the standpoint of practical reason the deduction is not really complete: It shows that there must be a practical viewpoint; but that conclusion itself requires a can-argument, since the practical viewpoint has to include the material of the faculty of desire, which imposes conditions that have so far not been taken into account. This can-argument *is* supplied in Chapters 2 and 3, but not in the Deduction itself.

Now, in one sense the Deduction does contain a complete argument since it argues that the will *must* be free (because of the Fact) and that it *can* be free (if we switch our viewpoint from theoretical to practical). But since its can-step is itself a must-step that requires further arguments, there remains a sense in which the deduction requires the arguments of Chapters 2 and 3.

These difficulties point to the fact that we need a much clearer understanding of the distinction between a deduction and a transcendental argument. I will not go into this question any further here, however, since for our purposes it is enough to see what the deduction establishes and what still needs to be established.

It should be pointed out, however, that the deduction here seems to perform a function that has no parallel in the first Critique: What this deduction establishes is the necessity of a practical viewpoint, whereas the first Critique could presuppose the theoretical viewpoint as given. This extra difficulty would find a parallel in the first Critique only if it were required there to first establish the factuality of experience before it could be used to ground the argument.

With this clarification of approach we can now turn to the text of the Deduction. I have divided my account of the argument into two parts corresponding to Kant's reference (at 46) to an exposition and a deduction proper.

The Exposition (KpV 42—46)

The Exposition begins with a recapitulation of the argument of the Analytic up to this point that at the same time makes clear what remains to be shown. Pure reason has "shown itself" to be practical through a fact (41—2). That fact has been shown to be "inextricably bound up with" (read: "analytically linked with") freedom (*ibid.*). So there really must be a pure will and that will must be free.

But the proof of the reality of a pure will does not change the fact that the will that acts is an empirically conditioned will—it is a rational faculty of desire. That will may be determinable by a law of pure reason, but it can only act on that law insofar as it has adopted the law into its maxim; and maxims are subjective principles, which means they are expressions of natural causality and always stand in a necessary relation to the faculty of

desire, whose necessity is not a rational necessity ("...the will of a
rational being, as belonging to the sensuous world, recognizes itself to be,
like all other efficient causes, necessarily subject to the laws of
causality..."— 42).

So it remains to be shown how the will *can* be free. This is the task of
the Deduction, and its method is to develop the notion of a *realm* of
freedom: "...for it has been sufficiently proved in another place that if
freedom is attributed to the will it transfers us into an intelligble order
of things" (42). (The "other place" is both the solution to the third
Antinomy and the argument of Chapter III of the *Groundwork*.)

Explicating this "intelligible order" and its relation to the phenomenal
order is the central concern of the Exposition. The question that lies behind the notion of an intelligible order is the question of our right to a
practical *viewpoint*—that is, what is at stake is our right to view phenomena that occur in experience as organized according to principles other
than those of mere mechanism. Looking at the problem in these terms,
there are two points that emerge from the Exposition as conclusions to be
drawn from the Theorems: (1) There must be a practical viewpoint that
is objective and yet different from the theoretical viewpoint, and (2) both
the theoretical and the practical viewpoints refer to the same phenomena.

(1) The investigation is framed within observations on the difference in
the starting points of the theoretical and the practical Analytics—such
observations introduce the discussion (second paragraph of 42) and close
it (first paragraph of 46). The importance of the starting point is not simply procedural—rather, it raises the question of the difference between the
two viewpoints, particularly with respect to what is given and indisputable
in each of them. For theoretical reason what is given as transcendentally
first is intuition ("pure sensuous intuition...was the first datum that made
a priori knowledge possible," 42). The priority of inutition lies in the fact
that theoretical cognition is of objects that must be given, so any activity
of intellect apart from intuition is mere thought. As long as our concern
is with knowing objects (which, for a finite theoretical cognition, must be

given), there must be intuition corresponding to those objects; and intuition has priority over intellect inasmuch as it establishes the factuality of the cognition. Even the will, if considered as an object of theoretical cognition, would be subject to the same restriction—we could only know it insofar as it was given (or possibly given) in intuition. So the theoretical point of view is not distinguished from the practical simply by its objects—that is, the practical viewpoint does not include a different set of facts, if by "facts" we mean phenomena.

Nevertheless, the moral law does present us with one fact (though it is not phenomenal but rather a priori) that is "absolutely inexplicable ... from the whole theoretical compass of reason" (43). That fact is not an intuition but rather a "dynamic law that can determine [the will's] causality in the world of sense" (42). It therefore implies the reality of a peculiarly practical use of reason—and a practical viewpoint—that is not concerned with knowledge of given objects but rather with the production of objects. And the practical production of objects must be viewed as occurring according to rules different from those that govern theoretical reason: They are causal rules but are the expression of a causality that is not restricted to determination in prior time—that is, they are expressions of a *free* causality.

The rules of this causality are rules of reason that form a systematic whole. They are rules for the production of a systematic unity of objects, which means that they are rules for the production of a *nature* under the rule of reason (nature being, in the most general understanding of it, "the existence of things under laws," 43). So the moral law and the rules associated with it define a "supersensuous nature," which is reason's representation of a systematic unity under laws of pure reason—a "pure world of the understanding" (*ibid.*).

(2) Nevertheless, by these rules one refers to the world of phenomena. They are not rules for relating noumena but rather for relating phenomena. This way of relating phenomena refers them to their noumenal ground, but it does not eliminate their character as phenomena:

This law gives to the sensible world, as *sensuous nature*, the form of an intelligible world, i. e. , the form of *supersensuous nature*, without interfering with the mechanism of the former (43).

From the practical viewpoint phenomena are represented as related to one another according to laws of a noumenal world. But at the same time they remain phenomena and therefore must be related according to laws of phenomena. So from the practical viewpoint phenomena are not represented as actually *being* related according to practical rules but as *to be* so related: The practical viewpoint occurs within the horizon of the "ought," just as the theoretical viewpoint occurs within the horizon of the "is." Its facts are not given appearances but rather actual will-determinations.

But although the world of practice is a world that ought to be, it still contains the same, given phenomena that make up the theoretical world. The difference lies in the fact that those phenomena are viewed as grounded in noumena and as subject to noumenal laws. And this viewpoint has objective reality just as much as the theoretical viewpoint, because "we regard [supersensible nature] as the object of our will as pure rational beings" (44).

So the Exposition shows us that the Theorems imply the reality of an objective practical viewpoint. The viewpoint is objective because, on the one hand, it involves the representation of a possible nature that is the thought of a system of phenomena under rules of reason—rules that command with necessity (so it is not simply an impression of my own subjective faculties); and, on the other hand, it is announced in a (practical) *fact*—an actual will-determination that we can become aware of simply by representing our duty to ourselves (so it is not a mere thought that exists only for intellect but not for the will).

The fact that the practical viewpoint is objective immediately implies that it has as a correlate a *practical world*. But since that "world" consists of the same phenomena as the theoretical world, I think it is preferable to use the term "realm" to refer to the objective correlate of the practical viewpoint. Kant himself does not use the word "realm" in the Deduction (I have borrowed it from the third Critique—KU, Introduction, Section II). Instead, he speaks of an "archtypal world" (43) or a "super-sensuous nature" (*ibid.*). But the word "realm" is more apt, I think, since it allows us to speak of two different realms involving the same phenomena. It indicates that what is at stake is not a difference of phenomena but a difference of lawful authority—or, to use less legalistic language, what is at stake is the organization of phenomena according to principles other than merely mechanistic ones.

Once a practical realm has been established, there exist the preconditions (and the need) for a transcendental argument concerning practice. In particular, the claim that the laws of a supersensuous nature do not interfere with those of sensuous nature is so far merely an assertion. How the two sets of laws interact in the same phenomena remains to be explicated; that explication involves showing that the moral law is the supreme condition of all willing, which is the task of Chapters 2 and 3 of the Analytic.

The immediate task, however, is the deduction: The Exposition has shown the implications of the Theorems but has drawn no conclusions. We now need to see what can and what cannot be deduced, and in what sense and to what extent.

The Deduction Proper

I have already quoted one passage in which Kant unambiguously denies that the moral law is the demonstrandum of the deduction ("... this vainly sought deduction..."—47). But we can cure ourselves of the almost irresistible urge to look for such a deduction (in spite of Kant's disclaimer) only by making clear what such a deduction would mean and showing why it is impossible. (Beck, for example, acknowledges that the moral law is not, strictly speaking, the demonstrandum of the deduction, but he still reads the deduction as being in some sense aimed at justifying the law—cf. Beck 173—4. [6]) To show why the deduction of the moral law is impossible will turn out to mean showing why no deduction can be completed within the theoretical viewpoint. So, having shown that, we will need to see what adopting a practical viewpoint means for the argument, and we will need to see what remains to be proved concerning the practical viewpoint.

Without going into the question of how a transcendental deduction might differ from other parts of a transcendental argument, we can at least say that transcendental deductions are concerned with the justification of a priori syntheses. This holds true in the *Groundwork* (GMM 447), in the Dialectic of the second Critique (113), in the *Metaphysic of Morals* (MM 395), and in the *Critique of Judgment* (KU Section 30 ff.)—in each case the need for a deduction is associated with a question of a priori synthesis.

My claim, however, is that the real problem of a priori synthesis is not simply a problem of a priori predication or of the linking of concept to concept—it is, rather, a problem of the a priori relation of irreducibly distinct faculties. Such a priori relations are required for any objective framework, but they need justification since the faculties involved cannot be reduced to a common ground: To justify a relation between distinct faculties on *a priori* grounds means to show by the analysis of concepts that the functioning of one faculty is compatible with the functioning of the other faculty (that needs to be proved because it might very well be the case that they are not at all or only partially compatible—intuitions might be simply incapable of being brough to unity under categories, or desires might be intrinsically incapable of being limited by the moral law). But that cannot be accomplished by a single analytic argument, because the two functions are mutually irreducible—that is, we cannot prove that faculty *A as such* stands in some determinate relation with faculty *B*.

The must/can structure of transcendental arguments offers a way out of this difficulty: Instead of proving that the two faculties, according to their very concepts, are compatible with one another, we can argue (a) that there must be such a relationship between the two faculties (considering them according to their most general determinations and arguing either analytically or on the basis of fact) and (b) (on different grounds) that further, specific determinations of the faculty are compatible with such a relation.

In the case of the Analytic of practical reason the a priori synthetic relation (expressed in the moral law) that seems to need justification is between pure reason and the will (which, for us, is always a faculty of desire, even though for the purposes of the Theorems we abstract from the will's content and consider only its form—that is, we consider the will only as finite rational causality). The Theorems prove (by the Fact and by analytical arguments) that there must be an a priori relation between reason and the will. So our problem is to show how there can be such a relation.

If we approach the problem as a problem for *theoretical* reason then what we need to show is that such an a priori relation is compatible with the conditions of theoretical knowledge. Theoretical knowledge of the will requires treating the will through concepts, and since the theoretical knowledge in question is for the sake of a transcendental deduction those concepts will have to be pure concepts. That means that the will will have to be considered simply as a rational cause. Now, if we simply analyze the concept of rational cause it turns out that a rational cause can only be thought as an unconditioned cause (cf. GMM 447—8). But since theoretical knowledge requires (in addition to concepts) intuitions, the only concept of causality that can yield theoretical knowledge for us is the schematized concept, which is always conditioned. That is why Kant says that, in order to show how reason can determine the will a priori, we would have to be able to show "how the logical relation of ground and consequence could be used synthetically with another kind of intuition than the sensuous" (49) — which is impossible for theoretical reason.

So a transcendental justification of the a priori relation between reason and the will is not possible for theoretical reason. And it is important to note that from the theoretical viewpoint it actually makes no difference

whether the principle to be deduced is the moral law or freedom, since
if we ask what a priori relation between faculties is involved in the two
principles it turns out to be the same: Both principles presuppose the
same synthetic relation between pure reason and the will, and it is that
relationship that must be justified.

The conclusion of all this is that there can be no deduction, from a
theoretical viewpoint, of either the moral law *or* freedom. What the deduction shows is that we need to presuppose a practical viewpoint if we are to
justify an a priori relation between reason and the will.

But even though the deduction cannot be carried through from a theoretical viewpoint, before we proceed to the question of what the shift of viewpoint means for the argument we do need to be able to show that the concept of free causality is at least not a theoretically *impossible* concept.
This point does not really require an elaborate demonstration, since it is
simply a conclusion drawn from earlier arguments (primarily in the first
Critique), as Kant points out:

> The determination of the causality of beings in the world of sense
> can never be unconditioned, and yet for every series of conditions
> there must be something unconditioned, and consequently a
> causality that is entirely self-determining. Therefore the idea of
> freedom as a faculty of absolute spontaneity was not just a de-
> sideratum but, *as far as its possibility was concerned*, an
> analytic principle of pure speculation (48).

(This same argument is given, in somewhat more detail, in the *Groundwork*—GMM 447—8.) The argument of the Antinomies showed that unconditioned causality was impossible for phenomena, but at the same time it
established the necessity of *thinking* such causality (otherwise there would
have been no antinomy). The section following the Deduction in the second
Critique adds one further link in this argument: There Kant claims that
the deduction in the first Critique not only justified the categories (and
among them the category of causality) for knowledge of objects of experience, but also justified their objective reality—apart from the restrictions
of our intuition—for objects (Objekte) *in general*:

The objective reality of the concept remains and can even be used with reference to noumena, though it is not in the least theoretically determined, and no knowledge can be effected with it (54).

So the Fact of the moral law "is a sufficient substitute for any a priori justification, since theoretical reason had to at least assume the possibility of freedom in order to fill one of its own needs" (47—8). The question of how pure reason *can* determine the will is still not answered, but the possibility of such a determination is shown to be at least a necessary thought for pure (speculative) reason and is to that extent rendered theoretically intelligible.

In addition, the concept of free causality is a practically necessary presupposition (since the determination of our will by pure reason is a practical fact). But that means that we are justified in asserting the objective reality of freedom for practical cognition only if we grant the validity of an objective practical viewpoint. So the "failure" of the deduction theoretically requires us to change the framework within which the question is raised.

A change of framework means a change in the faculties that determine knowledge: If we adopt a practical viewpoint we are' now no longer concerned with given intuitions being brought to the unity of consciousness under concepts but rather with will-determinations being brought to the unity of a pure will under practical principles.

The switch in viewpoint means that concepts are given meaning (Bedeutung) and referred to an objective realm *not* by virtue of their relation to intuition but by virtue of their relation to the will: It is no longer a question of supplying an intuition for the concept of rational causality but rather of supplying a will-determination; and that is done by the Fact of pure practical reason. (So from the practical viewpoint it *does* make a difference whether we take the moral law or freedom as what is to be deduced—it is only the moral law that, in immediately determining the will, supplies an actual will-determination for the concept of rational causality.) Kant sums this point up at the end of the Deduction:

> As to the concept that reason forms of its own causality as
> noumenon, reason need not determine it theoretically with a
> view to the cognition of its supersensible existence so as to
> give it significance (Bedeutung) in this way. For it acquires
> significance (Bedeutung) apart from this, though only for
> practical use, namely, through the moral law (49—50—
> Abbott's translation).

The concept has a determinate reference to objects, but not through intuitions. Instead, the reference is through the faculty of desire, as a
determination to produce objects.

So the question of the second step of the deduction—the question of how
pure reason *can* determine the will (which, from the theoretical viewpoint
became the question of how an intuition could be supplied for the concept
of unconditioned causality—a question that is theoretically insoluble)—
is answered by postulating a practical viewpoint within which the will's
causality is viewed as noumenally grounded (even though the will's effects
occur in the phenomenal world). From this viewpoint the entire natural
realm is seen as being subject to noumenal grounds—to a realm of freedom; and, correspondingly, the will's sensible conditions must, from
this viewpoint, be seen as subject to the pure will and its law (the moral
law).

The completion of the deduction, then, is accomplished by a switch to
a practical viewpoint. This viewpoint is a necessary presupposition if we
are to account for the Fact of pure practical reason and the conclusion
that must be drawn from the Fact, namely, that the will must be free.
But we have arrived at the conclusion that we must adopt a practical viewpoint through arguments that consider the will solely as finite rational wi
and that do not take into account the specific character of the will's sensi
bly conditioned nature: We have shown that the will must be viewed as a
member of a realm of freedom, but we have not shown how that realm ca
be a systematically unified objective realm. This second task involves
showing (to the satisfaction of practical reason) how the same phenomena
can be (at one and the same time) subject to different objective framewor

so that what is in one framework objective is in the other framework subjective, and vice versa) and how the one can be subordinated to the other.

Chapters 2 and 3 are concerned with this latter task, and they can therefore be seen as completing the argument of the Deduction, since they show how the unity of a practical framework is possible (which had to be presupposed in the deduction). So Chapters 2 and 3 are not concerned with new and different problems; instead, the whole Analytic can be said to have the structure of a set of "nested" arguments, with the second and third chapters serving to show how the realm established in the first chapter is possible (and doing so by explicating the conditions imposed on the will by its sensible nature).

The will's sensible nature is expressed in the fact that it is always conditioned by the material content of its willing. That content—treated up to this point as more or less monolithic—must now be considered in two different aspects, as objective material and as subjective material, in order to see what conditions it imposes on willing and to show how—in spite of these heterogeneous conditions—the realm of freedom is possible as a unitary objective realm. The objective and subjective material content of the will represent not simply correlative features of the will's content but rather successive levels of abstraction from the materiality of the will's object: If we abstract from the sensible content of the will's object (its relation to pleasure and pain) we can consider the object simply as an effect of the will's causality and therefore can deal solely with the practical understanding and its reference to objects. That is the abstraction that is made in Chapter 2—an object is simply an "effect possible through freedom," and the faculty of desire is simply a faculty of causality through representations. In Chapter 3 the object is considered in relation to sensibility and the special conditions that it imposes on willing. It is only with Chapter 3 that the possibility of the objective realm of freedom is fully secured.

Chapter 2 is concerned with the objective material content of the will (i.e., the will's material content insofar as it is subject to concepts), and its task is to show that the moral law, in determining the will, is the supreme condition of all the will's objective material content. This is not a new task but rather a continuation of the task of the Deduction, which adduced the will's existence in an "intelligible order of things"— an order that consists of laws of reason in authority over laws of nature and applying to natural phenomena—as a condition of the possibility of the will's being free. In particular, Chapter 2 is a continuation of the "can"-argument of the Deduction, since it turned out that the ultimate ground of the intelligible order—free causality—could not be rendered wholly comprehensible, but that nevertheless we must still enquire how such an order is possible in view of the conditions imposed by the will's membership in a sensible order (which is expressed by the will's being determinable by objects as well as by the law of pure reason).

The problem that remains for Chapter 2 is that the will's determinability by objects might impose conditions on willing that are incompatible with its membership in an objective intelligible order: It is not enough to prove (as Chapter 1 did) that the moral law immediately determines the will, since the will is also determinable by the representation of objects and there is no guarantee that these two modes of determining the will can cohere in one will and produce a reference to the same objective realm. It is at least thinkable that the two different modes of determining the will (since they are subject to different authorities—reason's and nature's) are in fact incompatible and might render impossible reference to a unified objective realm of freedom. To show that that is not the case we need to show that the concept of an object of the will can have univocal reference. That problem appears as the problem of establishing a univocal meaning for the good in which virtue is the supreme condition of happiness.

The argument occurs in two steps that, as in Chapter 1, conform to the must/can structure developed in the preceding chapters. The first step

(57—64) is primarily concerned with the supremacy of the moral good. It argues that the moral good *must* be the supreme good (i. e., the only unconditioned good and that which first determines the good per se and to which all other goods are a priori subject), and it does so by an argument that (once its premisses have all been spelled out) turns out to be analytic and to be based on the conditions of the possibility of an objective realm of freedom. (In particular, it is based on the conditions of the possibility of objective practical reference.) But that argument presupposes the systematic objective unity of the realm of freedom. So the second step (65—71) must show how that objective unity is possible. The solution is that it is possible through a single set of categories of freedom that express at one and the same time rational and natural necessity: These categories are what make possible the willing of a sensible object under a moral condition. But since they are not, strictly speaking, moral categories (rather, they are categories of willing in general through which objects can be willed under either sensible or nonsensible conditions), it remains to be proved [in the Typic (67—71)] that even in the case when the categories are willed under a nonsensible condition (i. e., as moral categories) they are capable of having a sensible content (an "application" to sensible objects). This is done by showing that the categories of freedom willed as moral categories are still categories of a nature in general (which have their seat in pure understanding) as are the categories of physical nature.

It is by no means arbitrary that there are these two distinct steps in the argument. We need to prove in Chapter 2 that the moral good objectively conditions the sensible good (from the viewpoint of practical reason). That proof requires an appeal to some realm of objective fact, and since experience will not serve the purpose, the appeal must be to a realm of freedom and the conditions of its possibility. This sort of appeal has in common with an appeal to experience a lack of perspicuity: It can only show that y must be the case because x is the case and y is a necessary condition of x. But since in the process of the proof reason must operate with material that it does not itself supply (in this case, material of the faculty of desire), it is always possible that in the transition from x to y the change in the material content of the judgment has introduced new conditions—unknown to reason—that in fact vitiate the proof. Thus if we argue that a necessary presupposition of a realm of freedom as a systematic unity of phenomena under laws of freedom is the a priori conditioning of the sensible good by the moral good, then we still cannot be certain without a further argument that that a priori conditioning is really possible. To see the latter we need to examine how the will actually refers to objects in this realm and thereby show how the moral law can condition objects a priori. So the proof of the first step actually requires, and in some sense presupposes, the elucidation provided by the second step.

Step 1: The Moral Good Must Be the Supreme Good

Kant begins with a paragraph that seems to be concerned simply with clarifying terms. But it is immediately followed by this paragraph:

> The sole Objects of a practical reason are thus those of the *good* and the *evil*. For, by the first, one understands a necessary object of the faculty of desire, and by the latter a necessary object of aversion, both, however, according to a principle of reason (58).

The impact of this paragraph is that the fundamental concept of an object of practical reason (i.e., what it means to be such an object) must be, on the highest level, univocal. This is, I think, the premiss of the first step, and I think Kant arrives at this premiss through an analysis of the opening explanation of what it means to be a concept of practical reason.

The first sentence of the chapter, "By a concept of practical reason I understand the representation of an object as an effect possible through freedom" (57), amounts to a presentation of the concept in "transcendental determinations"—that is, "in terms belonging to the pure understanding, i.e., categories, which contain nothing empirical" (9n—cf. KU Section 10). Not only does this Erklärung not contain any empirical concepts (a first requisite of an Erklärung for a transcendental argument)—

it abstracts from the difference between sensibly conditioned objects and objects of pure practical reason: Both are equally "effects possible through freedom."

And yet this Erklärung is not an arbitrary definition; it is simply a reformulation, in terms of pure concepts of the understanding, of the results of Chapter 1: There it was proved that pure reason is a cause and that therefore the will is free. The effects of such a cause must, therefore, be effects possible through freedom.

This Erklärung, then, is of a concept of practical reason *in general*, and the first step of the argument of Chapter 1 is an analysis of the consequences of this Erklärung. It is taken for granted in this first step that there *can be* such concepts; *how* there can be such concepts is considered in the second step.

If the notion of a concept of practical reason does have univocal reference to objects, then we can assign to the objects of these concepts the names good and evil, and these can be said to be the "*sole* objects of practical reason." These objects are effects possible through freedom, and they can be effects only through our faculty of causality, that is, through the faculty of desire (using again, a transcendental definition—this time of "faculty of desire"—namely, "the faculty such a being [viz., a living being] has of causing, through its representations, the reality of the objects of these representations"—9n). So the second paragraph is really a conclusion drawn from the first paragraph, and it asserts the premiss of the first step of the argument.

From this understanding of what it means to be a concept of practical reason we can derive two critieria for objective reference of practical concepts: In order to refer to an object in an objective practical realm a concept must (1) relate immediately to an actual desire as content and (2) refer to its content through rational determinations. If the first condition is lacking, then the concept does not refer to an object in the only way relevant for practice, namely, through a will-determination, and so it does not have reference to practical objects at all (although it could possibly be

given such a reference by additional representations). If the second condition is lacking, then the concept does not refer to an *objective* practical
realm but only to an individual subject. The first criterion is the requirement of immediate reference, and the second criterion is the requirement
of necessary reference.

In order to understand these criteria better it is helpful to draw
analogies with corresponding features of theoretical cognition. For theoretical cognition the problem of objective reference is the problem of
the reference of concepts to natural objects. And the rubric describing
the two necessary components of the reference-process is "concepts
without intuitions are empty, intuitions without concepts are blind" (cf.
KrV A51/B75). The requirement that concepts be given intuitional content
corresponds to the requirement of immediacy of reference in the practical realm, since for theoretical cognition it is only through intuition that
an object can be given. The theoretical requirement that intuitions be
united under concepts corresponds to the practical requirement of necessary reference.

With respect to the first requirement, in theoretical cognition the problem is to show how concepts—which have their seat in the pure understanding—refer to objects that must be presented in intuition (since, for theoretical cognition, it is only experience that has the immediate certainty
of a fact). But in the second *Critique* the problem is significantly different, and the difference relates to the fact that practical knowledge—unlike
theoretical knowledge—is not in the first place a species of the genus representation. The phenomenal territory of practical cognition is the same
as for theoretical cognition—the objects that we will to produce are also
objects of experience; and the practical reference to those objects does
also involve representations of intuition and of the understanding. But
ultimately practical knowledge is grounded in a determination of the will:

> To be an object of practical knowledge as such signifies, there-
> fore, only the relation [read: "relatedness"] of the will to the
> action whereby it or its opposite is brought into being (57).

So what plays the role corresponding to that of intuition in theoretical knowledge is desire, where by "desire" we mean here not the determination of our receptivity (pleasure or pain) but the determination of our causality: A practical concept has objective reference only insofar as it has a material content of desire (in the transcendental meaning of desire). Any practical concept that does not have such a content, and can only be given a content by virtue of further representations, cannot be said to refer to an objective realm of practical reason.

[It is important to notice here that the material content that is required for objective reference is *not* a specific object of the will but rather the determination to produce an object. It is true that the will cannot act to produce an object unless it has a determinate object as its goal, but nevertheless the will-determination comes first. The whole point of Kant's long digression in this chapter on the "confusions of philosophers" (64) is that the determination of a specific object is a later question, and that the objective reality of practical concepts is determined by the possibility or impossibility of willing the action. So a reading of Chapter 2 that interprets its aim as being to determine an object for the will misses the chapter's real point, which is the will's reference to an objective realm in general, not to some determinate object.]

With reference to the second criterion, in addition to material content, objective reference of concepts requires rational necessity. Here the analogy between theoretical and practical cognition is closer. In the case of theoretical cognition intuitions can only become knowledge insofar as they are brought to an a priori objective unity under concepts—otherwise they are "blind"—they attest to the determination of the subject by *something* (which cannot be called an object), but they do not yet refer to an *objective realm*. Likewise in practical cognition desire can refer to an objective realm only insofar as it involves a conceptual determination and ultimately a necessary unity.

From these considerations we can conclude that any concept of the good that (1) does not immediately contain an actual desire (will-determination) or (2) does not represent that desire under rational, necessary determinations lacks reference to an objective practical realm.

These two criteria are, I think, the foundation of Kant's argument for the supremacy of the moral good. His method is to show that the sensible good cannot, on any interpretation, meet both of these criteria, whereas the moral good can. So since these are criteria for the objective reference of a practical concept *as such*, the moral good must be what first supplies a determinate concept of the good. It is therefore in the objective practical realm the supreme condition of all good and that for the sake of which (in the judgment of reason) all good must be willed.

First Kant considers the possible identification of the good with the pleasurable. If the good were taken as what immediately pleases or causes pain, then—since pleasure and pain can determine desire immediately— the first criterion would be fulfilled: The judgment that x is good would have immediate reference to a material content. But in that case the real content can only be "the feeling of pleasure or displeasure as a receptivity belonging to inner sense" (58). This feeling is fundamentally subjective: It refers not to an object but to a state of the subject, as was argued in the second Remark to Theorem III (26). The faculty of feeling can never supply any but a subjectively necessary content, and (unlike intuition) it has no objectively necessary formal conditions—that was the "most important distinction that can be considered in practical investigations" (*ibid.*). Kant presents the argument summarily by noting simply that good or evil must be "judged by reason through concepts, which alone can be universally communicated, and not by mere sensation, which is limited to individual subjects and their receptivity" (58). And he points out that pleasure cannot be associated with an object a priori but rather only empirically (*ibid.*). The conclusion of this argument is that if the concept of the good were identified with the-pleasurable it would not refer to an objective practical realm.

Next Kant considers the interpretation that would call the good that
which is the *means* to pleasure (or to avoiding pain). Considered this way,
the good would involve rational necessity, since "reason alone is capable
of discerning the connection of means and purposes" (58). The second
criterion would thus be satisfied. But in that case the good would always
be only the means to something else—"the good would be only the useful"
(59)—and therefore "there would be nothing immediately good" (*ibid.*).
So the concept of the good as means to pleasure fails to satisfy the first
criterion, the criterion of immediacy.

If the fundamental reference of the concept of the good is dependent upon
the concept's relation to an object, then these two cases exhaust the possi-
bilities for what determines the good—it must be either the pleasurable or
the means to the pleasurable—and in neither case does the concept refer
to an objective practical realm (instead, it refers in both cases only to the
sensible world). So the good as such—that which is the objective referent
of a concept of practical reason in general—cannot be grounded on pleasure
or pain. Instead its ground must be the form of the action:

> ... it could not be a thing but only the manner of acting, i. e., it
> could be only the maxim of the will and consequently the willing
> person himself as a good or evil man (60).

The form of action that can serve as the fundamental determination of
the good is given by the moral law, since the law both is a product of
reason and determines the will immediately. So the moral law is the
fundamental condition of the possibility of objective reference in the practical realm:

> ... the moral law is that which first determines the concept of
> the good—so far as it absolute deserves this name—and makes
> it possible (64).

So in the objective judgment of reason the good as such can only be
accordance with the moral law—virtue—and the sensible good (which is
nevertheless an unavoidable component of the good for finite beings) can
only be willed under the condition of its accordance with virtue.

Step 2: The Moral Good Can Be the Supreme Good

Step 1 has argued analytically from the presupposition of the unity of
the practical realm with respect to objects and has concluded that since
the good must be a univocal concept it can only be the concept of happiness subordinated to virtue. The initial presupposition—the objective
unity of a practical realm—was not hypothetical; rather, it was the conclusion of the Deduction, which showed that the reality of such a realm
is a necessary presupposition of the moral Fact, which is itself immediately certain. So it would seem that it has been apodictically established
that the concept of the good is univocal and includes the moral good as the
supreme condition of all goods.

But although it does seem to have been shown that the concept of the
good *must* be univocal, with the moral good being the supreme good, nothing has been done to show how that is *possible*. In particular, the crucial
step of the argument was performed by concept analysis: Since there must
be an objective realm, and one condition of an objective realm is systematic unity under concepts, therefore the concept of an object of practical
reason must be univocal. This mode of arguing is in one way compelling,
but it does not take into account the particular nature of what is being
subjected to an objective unity—namely, that it is a faculty of desire,
which refers to objects as effects of its own causality. (The argument also
does not take into account the subjective determining grounds of the faculty
of desire—pleasure and pain—but that problem is dealt with in Chapter 3
of the Analytic.) The will's effects are products of a causality that is both
free and sensibly conditioned—it is a noumenally grounded causality (a
causality whose highest ground of determination must be posited not among
phenomena but among noumena), but it is also a cause in the natural world.
By positing a noumenal determining ground we do not eliminate the sensible conditions on the will's causality, we only maintain that those conditions do not necessarily *determine* its causality. So since the sensible conditions remain—and, in fact, the will cannot represent an object to itself

except as an *effect*—we need to see how it is possible for natural causality to coexist in one will with and be subordinated to noumenally grounded causality.

This question actually has two sides: One is from the point of view of our causality—How can a practical concept be both noumenally grounded and sensibly conditioned? The other is from the point of view of the effects of our causality: Since we inevitably will both happiness and virtue, how can we expect both effects to arise from our causality? This latter question is the question of the Dialectic, and it involves showing that it is at least not impossible that happiness occur in proportion to virtue. But that question is part of the question of the specification of a determinate object of the will (the problem of "finding an object"), and it does not concern us here. Here we are concerned with the possibility of the willing itself, granted that it involves both free and natural conditions.

It should also be noted that the question of possible unity that we are concerned with is not a question of the possibility of empirical conflict between sensible and moral determinations of the will. That sort of disunity is of course always possible (and perhaps even inevitable). To explicate the possibility of the objective unity of the practical realm is not to explain away the possibility of moral conflict, but rather to show how the moral law even has any relation to sensibly conditioned actions, granted that the two grounds of determination are irreducibly distinct. To put the question in slightly different terms, the possibility that must be eliminated is that there might be causal determinations of the faculty of desire that can have *no relation* to the moral law (that is, in principle, not simply in fact, since of course there will always be many particular desires that have no moral dimension at all). Instead we must show it is possible a priori for all desires to be objectively subject to the moral law.

The Categories

The introduction of the practical categories does not have the appearance of being a step in the argument because the categories are presented as requiring no justification—they "immediately become cognitions" (66). Worse yet, the categories seem to presuppose precisely the point that we are expecting an explanation of: By presenting a single set of categories for moral and sensible will-determinations Kant seems to take it for granted that all sensible conditions are a priori subject to the moral law. So what we need to show is (1) that the practical categories, as they are presented, do not presuppose an explanation of the possibility of the a priori subjection of sensible conditions on willing to the moral law, and (2) that the categories are a necessary step of such an explanation. [8]

(1) Both the fact that the categories do not presuppose what needs to be shown and the fact that they do not need justification result from a double abstraction under which the argument operates. On the one hand, throughout the chapter we abstract from the will's sensible content, and the faculty of desire is considered solely under the categories of cause/effect (so no question arises of a synthetic relationship between intellect and sensibility and therefore there is no need for a justification of such a synthesis). And, on the other hand, an abstraction is made from the noumenal grounding of the categories. This second abstraction is indicated by Kant's twice saying that the categories are categories of "practical reason in general" (66, 67), not of pure practical reason. So both pure reason and sensibility have been abstracted from, and the categories as first presented are categories simply of the practical understanding.

With that double abstraction in mind, and in order to see why the categories do not presuppose what is to be proved and why they do not need justification, we can fruitfully raise the question of what these practical categories are. Categories in general are a priori unity-functions. Theoretical categories are unity-functions for a manifold of intuitions. Practical categories are unity-functions for a "manifold of desires" (65). But, because of the first abstraction, the manifold is not considered here as a

sensible manifold: A manifold of desires is a manifold of causal determinations (not, for example, of pleasures). This abstraction is, of course,
not arbitrary—it is grounded in the fact that the will (unlike the faculty of
desire) is not determinable immediately by the representation of objects
as pleasurable: "... for the will is never determined immediately by the
object and our representation of it; rather, the will is a faculty for making
a rule of reason the motive for an action (through which an object can be
made actual)" (60—part of this sentence is omitted in Beck's translation).
So the synthesis of the practical categories *presupposes* a synthesis of
sensible determinations (pleasures) into causal determinations (desires);
but what this synthesis is itself concerned with is bringing those causal
determinations to an a priori systematic unity.

   These causal determinations, or desires, are representations of my
own causality without regard to the possible sensible determining grounds
of that causality. The function of the practical categories is to allow these
causal determinations to be willed together as determinations of a unitary
will that is not sensibly determined (a pure will). But because of the second abstraction that is made—the abstraction from a possible noumenal
determining ground—the categories do not present the pure will itself as
the determining ground of the causality that it serves to unify. In fact, the
question of the will's determining ground is left wholly out of consideration, and the sole question of the categories is whether a given action is
possible with respect to the unity of a will that is not determined by immediate pleasure.

   The unity in question is the systematic unity of a causal faculty. Since
causality is a category of the pure understanding, the unity that can be
supplied by practical categories will be that of systematic unity under
categories of the pure understanding—that is, it will be the unity of a
possible nature (67). But since the nature in question is not a mechanistic
nature, the categories of the understanding must be "taken so universally
that the determining ground of the causality can be placed beyond the
world of sense" (*ibid.* —note that Kant says only that the determining

ground *can* be placed beyond the world of sense). It is possible for Kant to take the categories in this "universal" sense because he can use the preschematized categories, which—as he pointed out earlier—were deduced in the first *Critique* for objects in general and therefore for a nature in general:

> This gives them a place in the pure understanding from which they are referred to objects in general, whether sensuous or not (54).

So the categories are categories for representing an action as occurring in a nature that is not determined mechanistically—according to the conditions imposed by inner sense—but rather rationally—according to the unity of the pure understanding itself. Whether the represented unity of the will is the ultimate determining ground of the action is left wholly out of account. The categories are therefore categories of freedom, but only in the negative sense that they represent the will as a causality whose determining ground is not immediately the sensible world. The will that makes use of these categories could nevertheless be determined by the idea of happiness, which—although it presupposes a material content and therefore experience—also requires understanding for the determination of its object: Pleasures can be compared on the level of intuition if the only question is their quantity; but for rationalizing desires into a systematic course of life these categories of freedom are required.

Because the categories are not, on the one hand, categories for the synthesis of pleasures, and are not, on the other hand, categories for the subjection of will-determinations to a noumenal determining ground, they do not require a transcendental justification and they do not presuppose the possibility of an a priori subjection of sensibly conditioned will-determinations to a pure moral law. Kant concentrates on the former point, arguing that because practical categories have as their immediate content instances of causality (in abstraction from sensibility), they do not need to "take over" their content "from sensibility" (66). So the problem that arose for theoretical cognition (which created the need for a deduction) does not arise here.

But the second point is equally important: If we ignore Kant's claim that the categories are categories of practical reason in general, then we will inevitably expect a justification of their placing the determining ground of the will's causality in pure reason. Such a justification is given—in the Typic—when the question is raised how these categories could function as moral categories. But it is important that the categories are first presented as conditions of the possibility of *all* willing, not just of moral willing. Even when an action is willed under a sensible condition (i. e., for the sake of happiness) it presupposes categories through which the will's causality in this action is brought into systematic unity with itself as productive of a course of life. This use of the categories presupposes a reference to an a priori ground of the will's unity (just as empirical theoretical cognition presupposes a reference to an a priori ground of unity in the knowing subject), but that ground is not therefore represented as the determining ground of the action. It is only the unconditioned use of the categories—where the action is willed as necessary solely because of the agreement of the maxim with the a priori conditions the unity of a will in general—that requires a transcendental justification.

(2) So these categories apply indifferently to all actions, good or bad, with the possible exception of actions performed for the sake of the moral law itself. These categories are as much conditions of the possibility of prudence as of morality, and they do not presuppose a determinate concept the good. But that means that the categories of freedom, on their first introduction—although they do not require justification—also do not solve the problem raised by the first step of the argument. That problem was to show how it is possible that every sensible condition on willing could be a priori subject to the moral law as supreme condition; and the most fundamental aspect of the problem was guaranteeing the unity of the will by guaranteeing that every sensible condition on willing stands in *some* a priori relation to the moral law.

The categories offer only a beginning to the solution of that problem: What they represent is the single set of categories through which any object must be willed (whether the object be purely moral or purely sensi‐ ble), once we grant that the will is (at least negatively) free. They are the categories of practical reason *in general*, and that fact is of central im‐ portance: The same categories are presupposed by (are conditions of the possibility of) all willing—moral willing differing from sensibly condi‐ tioned willing only in the *modality* of the willing ("the categories of modal‐ ity initiate the transition... from practical principles in general to those of morality..."—67). So the possibility of the unity of the will is based on the generality of the categories. That possibility can be *guaranteed* only by showing that in the case of moral willing—sensibly *unconditioned* willing—a sensible content can still stand in some relation to the pure will. That argument is the argument of the Typic.

The Typic

The whole of Chapter 2 operates under an abstraction: The chapter's subject matter is the material content of the will, but that material con‐ tent is considered in abstraction from its subjective component. That means that throughout the chapter we are concerned with the material of the will only as conceptually organized—we abstract from pleasure and pain and their relation to the faculty of desire. But the first part of the chapter also involves a second abstraction: The practical categories— although they are categories of freedom (which is a concept of reason) and therefore to that extent products of reason—are considered in abstrac‐ tion from their possible determination by pure reason. The categories are therefore considered as categories of practical reason in general, and as such they are conditions of the possibility of *all* willing, whether moral, nonmoral, or immoral.

But since our aim in this chapter is to establish the moral law as supreme condition of all the will's objective content (and, in particular, to show now *how* that is possible, since it has been proved that it *must b*

e case), we must now drop the second abstraction and consider the
ategories in the case when they are determined by the pure moral law.
ur purpose in doing that will be to show that all objective material con-
nt of the will is a priori subject to the categories as *moral* categories.
y saying that the will's objective material content is "a priori subject"
the moral categories I mean that the determination of the will's objec-
ve content as such presupposes the same synthetic function of judgment
at is presupposed by determination of the will by the moral law; and the
emonstration of that consists in the exhibition (not in intuition but rather
the understanding) of that pure a priori determination.

If the categories of freedom are employed under some sensible condi-
on (desire for some object) then no conflict arises between them and
atural necessity—any action that is chosen for the sake of some pleasure
perfectly capable of being subsumed under natural laws, and the func-
on of reason in that case is only to synthesize desires. The rules
overning reason's function in that case are homologous with those govern-
g its content. But if an action is chosen for its own sake ("if the reason
pure"—67) then its necessity cannot be subsumed under natural neces-
ty. It is subject to a law that is "a practical law, not a natural law be-
ause of empirical determining grounds but a law of freedom by which the
ll is determinable independently of everything empirical" (67—68). In
at case (since the will as phenomenon is always subject *also* to natural
ws) the will seems to be subject to two different laws and two different
cessitations, and "it seems absurd to wish to find a case in the world of
nse, and thus standing under the law of nature, that admits the applica-
n of a law of freedom to it" (68).

Kant's account of this difficulty involves showing the Schematism of the
st *Critique* as a parallel case. In the first *Critique* the difficulty was
at concepts (as functions of the pure understanding) had to be shown to
a priori "applicable" to intuitions (functions of sensibility). (The "ap-
ication" of categories to intuition means the presentation of intuitions
rough the synthesis of the concept.) That demonstration requires
hemata:

> The natural law, being a law to which the objects of sensible intuition as such are subject, must have a schema corresponding to it, that is, a general procedure of the imagination (by which it exhibits a priori to the senses the pure concepts of the understanding which the law determines) (69).

And in the Schematism those schemata are actually exhibited.

The fact that in Chapter 2 we have abstracted altogether from sensibility means that no schemata—strictly speaking—can be supplied for the practical categories; but neither are schemata required. The question of "application" here is not of the practical categories (under the moral law) to "actions as events in the world of sense" (68—we are not concerned with a synthetic relation between understanding and sensibility. Instead we are concerned with the relation between understanding and reason: The question is how categories of the practical understanding can be a priori subject to determination by pure reason. Transcendental imagination is therefore of no help here. Instead, the pure understanding itself must supply a pure formal representation that is homologous with, on the one hand, the sensibly conditioned use of the categories and, on the other hand, the moral law as a law of pure reason:

> Thus the moral law has no other cognitive faculty to mediate its application to objects of nature than the understanding (not the imagination); and the understanding can supply to an idea of reason not a schema of sensibility but a law, but one that can be exhibited in concreto in objects of the senses, consequently a natural law, only according to its form for the use of the faculty of judgment, and it may therefore be called the type of the moral law (69).

So what pure understanding supplies to the faculty of practical judgment is the thought of a law of nature represented in its purely formal aspect as lawfulness in general (that is, in abstraction from the conditions of a particular nature). That form of lawfulness can be presented in concreto through a natural law, but we must use the natural law only as a concrete presentation of lawfulness in general:

We are therefore allowed to use the *nature* of the *sensuous world* as the *type* of an *intelligible nature*, so long as we do not carry over to the latter intuitions and what depends on them but only apply to it the form of *lawfulness* in general (the concept of which occurs in the purest use of reason, though it cannot be known definitely a priori except with reference to the pure practical use of reason). For laws as such are all equivalent, regardless of whence they derive their determining grounds (70).

Hartenstein "corrects" the phrase "purest use of reason" in this passage to read "most common use of reason" (*reinsten* becoming *gemeinsten*), a correction that in a way makes sense and at least does not spoil the meaning. But it is important that there are three distinct levels on which the idea of lawfulness appears: (a) It is a representation of pure reason, on which level it represents purely rational necessity. (b) It is presupposed by the representation of nature in general through the categories as a systematic unity under laws. And (c) it can be presented in an actual (empirical) instance of causality according to laws, so that (indeed) the form of lawfulness *is* present even in the commonest use of reason. Point (c) is important, however, only as guaranteeing the presentational immediacy of the idea; it is the homology between (a) and (b) that is important for the argument, and for that reason Kant needs to emphasize the origin of the idea of lawfulness in *pure* reason.

Since both natural necessity and moral necessity presuppose the same pure form of lawfulness in general (which can be presented in concreto as well), the "applicability" of the moral law to actions is guaranteed a priori: There can be no sensibly conditioned will-determination that does not stand in an a priori relation to the moral law (through the pure form of lawfulness in general). So the categories of freedom—which, when considered in abstraction from their possible determination by pure reason, were conditions of the possibility of the willing of objects in general—can serve to bring a manifold of desires to the unity of the will even if that will is determined by the pure moral law (i. e., even if the categories are willed as practically necessary rather than contingent). That means that even though the manifold of desires (as a causal manifold) is necessarily subject to the lawfulness of sensible nature, there is no a priori conflict between that lawful authority and the authority of the moral law that could prevent the bringing of that manifold to the a priori unity of a pure will under the moral law.

The unity of the pure, morally determined will with respect to its objects is therefore guaranteed a priori, and along with it the objective unity of the realm of freedom under moral laws. That is, we have now shown how the moral law *can be* the supreme condition of all objects of the will in a practical realm. And, since in the first part of the chapter it was proved that the moral *must be* the supreme condition of the good, we can now say that the sensible conditions imposed on willing by the will's objective material content are, one and all, a priori subject to the moral law as supreme condition in the practical realm.

That does not mean that every action is *determined* by the moral law, but rather that every action is *determinable* by the moral law. (That is, once again, the question of the will's relation to objects is raised not on the level of empirical psychology but on the level of a transcendental enquiry into the conditions of the possibility of a realm of freedom; how or what the will actually chooses in that realm is left out of consideration.)

. . .

Chapter 2 as a whole has considered the will's material content only as *objective* material content. The unity of the realm of freedom and the supremacy of the moral law within that realm have thus been shown only under a restriction. The will is also subject to sensible conditions of pleasure and pain, and it remains to be shown how the moral law can be the supreme condition of these subjective determining grounds of the will. That is the task of Chapter 3.

7. THE ARGUMENT OF CHAPTER 3

Chapter 3 is concerned with the will's subjective material and the conditions that that material imposes on willing and on the possibility of the will's membership in a realm of freedom. Chapter 2 showed the *objective* unity of the realm of freedom (the will's univocal reference to objects), and Chapter 3 must now show the *subjective* unity of that realm—an aim that could also be stated as being to show the ultimate subjective grounds of unity of the willing subject.

The reason this needs to be shown is because of the peculiar nature of the moral law and the way in which it determines the will: The moral law determines the will immediately, without appealing to any sensible ground of determination. But the subjective unity of the will is grounded on the fact that the will's principles all stand in a determinate relation to the faculty of pleasure and pain—it is only insofar as a principle stands in such a determinate relation (only insofar as it has been *chosen*) that it can function as *my* maxim and determine my will (cf. Appendix D: Maxims and Laws). If the moral law determines the will, and therefore serves as a subjective determining ground, but does so without reference to pleasure or pain, then there would seem to be an internal contradiction in willing: The will would be determinable by a principle that stood in no relation to sensible determining grounds and therefore might not be capable of being brought into any sort of unity with them. The solution to this problem is to show that in immediately determining the will the moral law also determines the faculty of feeling, and that that determination brings other, sensible grounds of determination into a priori relation with the determination by the moral law—where the quality of that a priori relation is one of subordination and limitation.

This interpretation of the problem of Chapter 3 differs from the interpretation that sees the chapter as concerned with establishing a moral incentive as motive force for the law: The problem of the ultimate unity of the will's subjective determining grounds can only arise *after* it has been shown that the moral law must determine the will immediately. So

my interpretation not only does not recognize the "need" for supplying
the moral law with an incentive as motive force—it is precisely because
the law does *not* need a sensible incentive that a transcendental problem
arises.

That this is the real concern of the chapter is indicated, I think, by the
fact that Kant begins the chapter immediately with the assertion that
in moral willing the moral law must determine the will *directly*:

> What is essential in the moral worth of actions is *that the moral*
> *law immediately determine the will.* If the determination of the
> will occurs *in accordance with* the moral law but only by means of
> a feeling of any kind whatsoever that must be presupposed in order
> that the law may become a sufficient determining ground of the
> will, and thus occurs not *for the sake of the law,* the action has
> *legality* but not *morality* (71).

Having asserted that, Kant's next step is analogous to the first step of
the argument in Chapter 2: He provides an Erklärung of the concept of an
incentive that is designed to abstract from the *source* of the will-determination, so that both the moral law and sensible determining grounds
can be considered under the same concept:

> Now, if by an *incentive* ... we understand a subjective determin-
> ing ground of a will whose reason does not by its nature neces-
> sarily conform to the objective law, it follows, that the [moral]
> incentive of the human will (and that of every created rational
> being) can never be anything other than the moral law (72).

This Erklärung must be thought of not simply as an arbitrary definition,
but rather as part of the first step of the argument that sets up the problem of the chapter: If an incentive is any subjective determining ground,
and if the moral law determines the will directly and sufficiently, then
the moral law must itself be an incentive. Then our problem is to see
how *this* incentive relates to *sensible* incentives, as Kant says in the
second paragraph:

> Since, then, on behalf of the moral law and in order to try to give
> it influence on the will no further incentives must be sought ...
> therefore nothing remains but to determine carefully in what way
> the moral law becomes an incentive, and, since the moral law
> is such an incentive, to see what happens to the human faculty of
> desire as a consequence of this determining ground (72).

Even this formulation of the chapter's aims could be misinterpreted as seeming to claim too much (as Kant recongizes): We know that the moral law *must* be an incentive, but we cannot explain *how* it can be an incentive. To explain that would require showing how pure reason can be a cause:

> For how a law in itself can be the immediate determining ground of the will (which is the essence of morality) is an insoluble problem for the human reason. It is identical with the problem of how a free will is possible. Therefore we shall not have to show a priori why [den Grund woher] the moral law in itself supplies an incentive but rather what it effects (or, better, must effect) in the mind, so far as it is an incentive (72).

The framework within which the enquiry occurs once again seems to be the distinction between an argument showing that something *must* be the case and an argument showing how it *can* be the case. And with respect to the a priori (synthetic) relation between reason and the faculty of pleasure and pain, Kant asserts that we can show what the relation *must* be, but we cannot show how it is possible—a situation perfectly analogous to that of the Deduction.

But, in fact, the impossibility is more than simply analogous: It is the very same impossibility that prevented us from carrying through the deduction of freedom (namely, the ultimate incomprehensibility for theoretical reason of causality determined by pure reason). For just that reason Kant's disclaimer does not have the sweeping implications for the chapter that it would seem to have. (It does not, for example, mean that the whole chapter will have to be in the form of a "must"-argument and therefore be wholly analytic.) The problem of Chapter 3 is a more restricted problem than that of the Deduction; it is a problem that remains after the impossibility of a complete deduction of the concept of freedom has been admitted—namely, the problem of showing how the subjective unity of the willing subject is possible, granted that the will is both immediately determinable by the moral law and necessarily conditioned by sensible determining grounds.

This explains why the argument is not—as we would otherwise expect—entirely analytic: If it were impossible to give any "can"-argument at all with respect to the moral law as incentive then we would be reduced to arguing only what *must* be the case. And in that case our arguments would have to be strictly analytic. But as it is, if we accept as given that the moral law *does* determine the will immediately, then we still need to give an argument showing the subjective grounds of unity of the will, and that argument will include both a must-argument and a can-argument.

The Division of the Chapter

The primary difficulty in interpreting the actual argument of Chapter 3 is that the same argument seems to be repeated over and over, which gives the impression that there is no logical progression. So it is especially important to show at the outset the over-all divisions of the argument in order to show that there are definite steps rather than simply constant repetition.

In the first place, the chapter can be divided roughly into two halves: The first half (71—81) contains the actual argument for the existence of an *interest* in morality; and the second half (81—89) develops the concept of the moral interest as *duty*, as distinguished from a (fantastic) love for the moral law, and shows that the basis of this distinction is the fact that the moral interest is grounded not on the (pathological) life-principle but rather on personality (as membership in an intelligible world). The latter half of the chapter is more elucidation of the concept of moral interest than strictly an argument, so it is the former half that we will be concerned with.

The first half of the chapter can likewise be divided into two parts: The first part (71—76) establishes the moral incentive (respect), and the secon part (76—81) establishes the moral *interest* based on that incentive that allows the moral law to be adopted into one's maxims.

Finally, the first part of the first half of the chapter is also divided into two steps: The first step (third paragraph) argues that there *must* be a moral feeling, and it does so by an analysis of the concept of a free will and the transcendental definitions of pleasure and pain; and the second step (fourth paragraph) shows, on the basis of the way objects relate to the will, how the moral feeling can be produced by the moral law. (This second step also includes a recapitulation of part of the first step, thus contributing to the appearance of repetitiveness.)

The Moral Feeling

The First Step

The first step in the argument occurs in a single paragraph (the third and fourth paragraphs in Beck's translation). This step is a "must"-step, and it is entirely analytic. It contains two distinct points, and these points are connected by a brief aside on self-love and self-conceit, which is an anticipation of the second step.

The two points proved in the first step are that

the moral law, as a ground of determination of the will, by thwarting all our inclinations, must produce a feeling that can be called pain (73)

and that

since this law is in itself positive, being the form of an intellectual causality, ... it is an object of the greatest respect and thus the ground of a positive feeling that is not of empirical origin (*ibid.*).

The proof of the first point is as follows: The moral law in determining the will rejects and checks all sensuous impulses. But all sensuous impulses are based on feeling, and a check on inclinations will itself be a feeling—namely, a feeling of pain. Therefore the moral law, in determining the will, must produce a feeling of pain. The last step in this argument is based on the transcendental definitions of pleasure and—by implication—of pain that Kant gives in the Preface:

Pleasure is the representation of the agreement of an object or an action with the subjective conditions of life, i.e., with the faculty through which an idea causes the reality of its object... (9n).

From this definition the last assertion follows analytically.

There is one element in the first part of the first step whose importance is not at first clear, namely, the claim that the moral law rejects *all* inclinations. In order to prove merely that there is a moral feeling of pain (at the thwarting of inclinations) Kant does not need the assertion that *all* inclinations are rejected by the law—even the rejection of a single inclination would be painful. But the peculiar character of the moral law's determination of the will is that it does reject all inclinations. And that becomes particularly important in connection with the positive feeling (respect for the moral law), since Kant needs ultimately to show that respect is like no other feeling: Respect is "not of empirical origin" (73), and the proof of that, in the second part of the first step, depends upon showing that the moral law rejects all inclinations.

What it means to reject all inclinations is not immediately obvious. The explanation of that and the argument showing how it is possible are not given until the second step. But since Kant needs the assertion to complete the first step of the argument, he introduces in an aside the concepts in terms of which the assertion must be formulated, namely, the concepts of self-love and self-conceit: "All inclinations taken together . . . constitute self-regard. This consists either of self-love or . . . self-conceit" (73). At this point the terms "self-love" and "self-conceit" are merely replacements for the concept of " inclinations taken together, " since that is all that is required for the second part of the first step.

The second point is argued as follows: The moral law determines our causality, so it is a positive power; and insofar as we are aware of that power through feeling (namely, through its limiting our self-love), we can be said to have a positive feeling produced by the law. And because the determination of the will by the moral law involves striking down self-conceit at its roots, the feeling it produces is not of empirical origin (since any empirically grounded feeling would only oppose one inclination to another, not reject all inclinations as determining grounds).

The conclusion to be drawn from these two points is that

> Respect for the moral law, therefore, is a feeling produced by
> an intellectual ground, and this feeling is the only one that we
> can know completely a priori and the necessity of which we can
> discern (73).

What remains unexplained is *how* the moral law rejects all inclinations
(and what it means to "limit self-love" and "strike down self-conceit").
That explanation is the task of Step 2.

The Second Step

The second step must show how the moral law can reject all inclinations. We cannot show the ultimate grounds of reason's determination of
the faculty of pleasure and pain, but we can see why that determination
has the character of a rejection of "all inclinations taken together"—that
is, a rejection of self-love and self-conceit.

This step, like the first, occurs in a single paragraph (the fourth). But,
as Kant presents it, it is so highly condensed and allusive that it requires a great deal of amplification and clarification. The basic argument
is, I think, synthetic, in the sense that it develops two different modes of
determination of the will and their presuppositions and shows their ultimate grounds to be in conflict. In particular, it shows that the determination of the will by sensible determining grounds presupposes an ultimate
ground of unity of the will that is different from that required on objective
grounds by the will's reference to objects, so that the unity of the will
requires the subordination of the former to the latter. To show that, we
must begin with an account of the nature of the determination of the will
by sensible determining grounds—an account that Kant only alludes to
here, although its elements can be found in Remarks I and II to Theorem
II in Chapter 1.

Inclinations are feelings of pleasure or pain regarded as determining
grounds of the will. As such they are the subjective expression of our
finite nature, i. e., of the fact that we are beings that are always conditioned by needs. But in order to determine the will inclinations must be

brought into systematic unity. The subjective ground and first presupposition of this unity is the pathological self, and its principle is the principle of self-love. Self-love is, then, in the first place, simply the name for the natural tendency of the (finite) will to refer all its determinations to the pathological self as subjective ground of unity of all desires (which is how Kant first defines self-love: "predominant benevolence towards oneself"—73). But even the representation of all inclinations as grounded in the pathological self requires a concept—namely, the concept of happiness. So the determination of the will by inclinations also presupposes a synthesis under concepts. This is why Kant introduces the notion of happiness in the aside in the first step: "All inclinations taken together (which can be brought into a fairly tolerable system, whereupon their satisfaction is called happiness) constitute self-regard" (73). (See also Remark II following Theorem II, 25f.: "The concept of happiness always underlies the practical relation of Objects to the faculty of desire." But a synthesis under concepts presupposes an objective *ground* of the synthesis. So the determination of the will by subjective determining grounds presupposes an objective ground of synthesis as well.

It is for that reason that Kant redefines self-love more precisely in Step 2 as a "propensity to make oneself according to the subjective grounds of one's Willkür into an objective determining ground of Wille in general" (74): The determination of the will by inclination presupposes the representation of the pathological self and the satisfaction of its needs under the concept of happiness, and that, in turn, presupposes an objective ground of unity, which in this case can only be the pathological self. This natural tendency to represent subjective determining grounds as objective is what is called self-love. And the perversion of this tendency (but which also has its roots in our nature, since the representation of any objective unity presupposes the representation of an ultimate, necessary unity) is self-conceit—the representation of subjective determining grounds not only as objective but as *necessary.*

Kant expresses this tendency of the will as follows:

> We find now, however, our nature as sensuous beings so
> characterized that the material of the faculty of desire
> (objects of the inclinations, whether of hope or of fear) first
> presses upon us; and we find our pathologically determina-
> ble self, although by its maxims it is wholly incapable of
> giving universal laws, striving to give its pretensions
> priority and to make them acceptable as first and original
> claims, just as if it were our entire self (74).

But this natural tendency is in opposition to the objective conditions of

unity of the will: In Chapter 2 it was proved that from the practical view-

point it is the moral law that first determines the objective practical

synthesis, and that sensible determining grounds under the concept of

happiness are a priori subordinated to the pure formal determination of

the will by the moral law. That proof implies that the ultimate practically

objective ground of unity of the will cannot be the pathological self but

must, rather, be the pure will. This conclusion is summed up by Kant in

the first sentences of the fourth paragraph:

> In the preceding chapter we have seen that anything that presents
> itself as object of the will prior to the moral law is exluded from
> the determining grounds of the will which is called unconditional-
> ly good by the law itself as the supreme condition of practical
> reason. We have also seen that the mere practical form, which
> consists in the competency of the maxims to give universal laws,
> first determines what is of itself and absolutely good... (73—4).

This means that there is an a priori opposition between the ultimate

ground of unity presupposed by subjective determining grounds and that

required by objective determining grounds. So if the will's unity is to be

preserved, the pathological ground must be subordinated to the pure

rational ground. And that subordination must be *a priori*—that is, the

opposition is not between particular sensible determining grounds and

particular rational determining grounds, but between sensible and rational

determining grounds *as such*. So the subordination that is required must

likewise be between those determining grounds as such. The moral law,

therefore, in determining the will does not reject *each and every* inclina-

tion: instead, it rejects the claim of inclinations *as such* to determine the

will—in determining the will immediately the moral law "disconnects" the ultimate ground of all sensible will-determinations (the pathological self) from the will.

This is the explanation of how it is possible for the moral law to reject all inclinations at once; or, as Kant says (after recapitulating the argument of Step 1):

> Thus we conceive how it is possible to understand a priori that the moral law can exercise an effect on feeling, since it blocks the inclinations and the propensity to make them the supreme practical condition (i. e., self-love) from all participation in supreme legislation (74).

These two steps have been designed to establish what Kant calls the "moral feeling." This feeling is in the first place an awareness of the blocking of all inclinations in the face of the moral law, and to that extent is simply a feeling of pain. But since the moral feeling results from the frustration of *all* pathological incentives as such, it is clear that it cannot originate in the senses, even though it is through the senses that we become aware of the force of the moral law. It is a feeling that "cannot be said to be pathologically effected; rather, it is practically effected" (75).

But as a positive feeling the moral feeling is even more peculiar: It is not a feeling *for* anything, nor is it a pleasure taken *in* any object. It is simply the recognition of the positive power of the moral law as a determining ground of the will, a power that is subjectively manifested *only* in the law's ability to "deprive self-love of its influence and self-conceit of its delusion" (75). So although the moral feeling is directed *to* the moral law (it is respect *for* the moral law) it is in no sense a liking to obey the law or a desire for morality:

> ...for this law there is no feeling, but, as it removes a resistance, this dislodgment of an obstacle is, in the judgment of reason, equally esteemed as a positive assistance to its causality (75).

So the term "moral feeling" refers only to the law's effect upon the faculty of feeling—the effect, namely, of recognition (even on the level of feeling) of the superiority of the moral law to all sensible incentives. But this feeling presupposes the determination of the will *solely* by the moral law. That is why Kant can say

Respect for the moral law is not the incentive to morality; it is morality itself, regarded subjectively as an incentive, inasmuch as pure practical reason, by rejecting all rival claims of self-love, gives authority and absolute sovreignty to the moral law (76).

This understanding of the moral feeling gives us a basis for understanding how the moral law can be adopted into one's maxims. That question is the question of the moral interest, which we must consider next.

The Moral Interest

The remainder of the chapter is concerned (directly or indirectly) with the moral interest; but the actual argument establishing the moral interest occurs in a single paragraph (78—9), and the remainder of the chapter is devoted to clarifying and underlining the peculiar nature of the moral interest (namely, that it is duty, which is always a constraint rather than pleasure, even though it is a self-imposed constraint). The reason for this emphasis on the nature of duty is not mere moral didactics, nor is it due to the fact that the moral interest is capable of being misrepresented as being a love for virtue. Instead, I think Kant emphasizes the point because it leads back to the question of the possibility of the will's membership in a realm of freedom, which is the unifying concern of the Analytic.

The argument showing what the moral interest must be is straightforward: It follows analytically from the nature of the moral incentive and from the meaning of the term "moral interest," and it has been prepared for by Step 2 of the argument.

Kant defines the term "interest" in a rather obscure way ("... an incentive of the will so far as it is presented by reason" 79). I think the reason he gives such an opaque definition is that he wants to include both the pathological and the moral interest in a single term. If we were concerned only with the pathological interest, then "interest" would simply be the technical term for an incentive that has been brought to an objective unity with the totality of the will's incentives under a concept of happiness—a notion that we made use of in clarifying Step 2 without actually using the term. This understanding of the term (so long as we restrict our consideration to pathological interests) is in keeping with the discussion of the term in the third *Critique*. There Kant defines "interest" as "delight we connect with the real existence of an object" (KU, Section 2); and later he clarifies that further:

> Such delight is determined not merely by the representation of an object, but also by the represented bond of connection between the subject and the real existence of the object (KU Section 5).

For practical reason that "bond of connection" is a causal rule determining the will under a concept of happiness. And causal rules presuppose more than just feeling—they presuppose reason. So the definition of an interest as "an incentive of the will so far as it is presented by reason" would include pathological interests, but it is framed in broad enough terms that it can also include the moral interest. In either case, what distinguishes an interest from an incentive is the presentation through reason.

In order to establish the nature of the moral interest Kant recapitulates the argument of Steps 1 and 2, emphasizing that "the acknowledgment of the moral law is the consciousness of an activity of practical reason on objective grounds" (79). That means that in the feeling of respect the moral law, as a product of pure reason, appears as the determining ground of the subjective feeling: It is the peculiar nature of the moral incentive that its source is objective rather than subjective (using the practical meaning of objectivity established in Chapter 2—namely, "based on the activity of reason rather than on determinations derived from sensibility"). That is, the moral incentive is recognized as being a product of reason rather than of sensibility.

So since an interest is an incentive so far as it is presented by reason the effect that the moral law has on the faculty of feeling in determining the will can be said to be the production of an immediate interest in the object of the law (virtue). The moral incentive, unlike pathological incentives, does not require any further objective determination in order for

he will to take an interest in it—the interest is immediate. And that
interest "must be a pure nonsensuous interest of the practical reason
lone" (79).

So the question of how it is possible for the moral law to be adopted into
ne's maxims is answered as follows: The moral law, in determining the
ill immediately, at the same time determines the faculty of feeling, and
1e effect the law has on feeling is such that it a priori negates the claims
f sensible conditions to determine the will. So without producing a liking
ir morality, the moral law determines the faculty of feeling as a whole
priori. The necessary condition of the moral law's being adopted into
ne's maxims—namely, that it be brought into a determinate relation with
ubjective determining grounds—is therefore fulfilled: The law stands in
n a priori relation to the faculty of feeling, and that relation is one of
ibordination of all sensible conditions as such to the pure law. That a
riori subordination is what Kant calls the moral interest.

But the interest that the will takes in virtuous acting is different from
1y pathologically effected interest since it involves absolutely no *inclina-*
on to do the action: The necessity of the action is always viewed as con-
:raint, because the moral law in determining the will excludes all in-
linations. The closest thing to pleasure that can be associated with the
1oral interest is the feeling of self-approbation (81). But even that is a
:eling that exists only insofar as the acting person "knows himself to be
:termined to the action solely by the law" (*ibid.*), so it involves no in-
lination to perform the action.

If it were not for the fact that the moral interest excludes all pathologi-
1l determining grounds, we would not be able to know anything about it
priori ("it would be futile to try to discover a relation of the feeling to
1y idea a priori" 80). As it is, we can show on pure a priori grounds
hat the relationship must be between reason and the faculty of feeling
1at allows the moral law to be adopted into one's maxims: That relation
an a priori determination of the faculty of feeling that excludes all in-
.inations from becoming determining grounds of action. So we now see

how the subjective unity of the realm of freedom is possible.

The rest of the chapter is devoted to a clarification of the notion of the moral interest as duty (a self-imposed constraint). The major point Kant makes is that the concept of duty must be kept free from any admixture of pleasure since, rather than strengthening the determination of the will, that undermines it. The reason for that is clear from the second step of the argument: The will has an unavoidable tendency to represent subjective determining grounds as objective determining grounds. But since the unity of the will requires that there be only a single ultimate determining ground, that misrepresentation involves undermining morality to its very root, since it makes the pathological self the ultimate ground of determination of the will.

There remains a fundamental difficulty in understanding how pure reason can determine the faculty of desire, and Kant brings the argument back to the point arrived at in the Deduction by pointing out that the moral interest reveals to us (subjectively) "our own supersensuous existence" (88). He arrives at this point by seeking out the root of the concept of duty, and that root is personality,

> i. e., the freedom and independence from the mechanism of
> nature regarded as a capacity of a being that is subject of
> special laws (pure practical laws given by its own reason), so
> that the person as belonging to the world of sense is subject
> to his own personality so far as he belongs to the intelligible
> world. For it is not to be wondered at that man, as belong-
> ing to two worlds, must regard his own being in relation to
> his second and higher vocation with reverence and the laws
> of this vocation with the deepest respect (87).

So the moral interest—like the concept of the good in Chapter 2—is a concept that is only possible in, and that at the same time makes possible, a realm of freedom.

So even though we cannot fully understand theoretically how free causality is possible, we do at least understand how—if we postulate a realm of freedom and a practical viewpoint corresponding to it—the conditions imposed on the will both objectively and subjectively by its material content are capable of subordination to the unity of a pure will whose supreme condition is the moral law. The arguments of Chapters 2 and 3 have not solved the problem of the Deduction in the sense of explaining to the satisfaction of theoretical reason how pure reason can determine the will; but they have shown how it is possible to adopt an entirely different—practical—viewpoint with respect to phenomena, and they have shown that that viewpoint is compatible with the will's existence as sensibly conditioned in the realm of nature.

PART III
CONCLUSIONS

8. CONCLUSIONS AND DISCUSSION

The Second Critique

The preceding three chapters have shown, I think, that the Analytic of the second Critique can be consistently read as a single transcendental argument establishing a practical framework within which the moral law is the supreme condition of all maxims, objects, and incentives (where the moral law's being the supreme condition of all willing is a condition of the possibility of a practical viewpoint but is not a condition of the possibility of willing). And I think this kind of reading of the argument is needed to account for all the otherwise seemingly disparate elements of the text.

In particular, other readings offer no way of accounting for the presence of Chapters 2 and 3 in the argument except by introducing the premiss that the will has a need for an object and an incentive that must be fulfilled if the will is to be able to act. But that sort of reading (besides actually contradicting the findings of Chapter 1) already presupposes a cognitive framework within which the question of an object or an incentive is raised— and, in fact, it presupposes a theoretical framework. What that sort of reading does is to reduce the transcendental questions about the will's objects and incentives to questions of empirical psychology.

Our reading, on the other hand (while acknowledging that, of course, the will always does have an object in acting, even in the case of moral willing), interprets the motivation for the inclusion of Chapters 2 and 3 as a need of practical reason. That is, on this interpretation, objects and incentives of the will (which are in any case present) must be shown to be capable of being brought to the unity of a pure will a priori, which is a very different problem.

So the argument makes sense, and at the same time can be seen as a single, continuous argument, if we are careful not to interpret the questions it deals with to be questions of empirical psychology: It is not with empirical objects or empirical incentives that the argument is concerned but with objects and incentives considered according to their transcendental Erklärungen—that is, objects and incentives insofar as they can be grasped under concepts of the pure understanding.

That means that the second Critique does not really deal with the extremely important (and problematic) question of how we determine (empirically) a particular action in a particular situation, granted that the moral law is a pure formal law and tells us nothing about particular actions. That problems is, of course, of great practical importance, but I do not think it is raised in the second Critique (except, in a very limited sense, in the Methodology). On the other hand, the *Metaphysic of Morals* does provide some help along those lines, since it begins the process of deriving more concrete duties from the moral law. But even there Kant's account is of only limited usefulness, since the question always remains of how *this* maxim (which expresses only what I will in general) applies to *this* situation. And that question is a quite serious one—all the more so since Kant's own applications of his principles sometimes seem highly suspect (for example, in the essay "On the Supposed Right to Tell a Lie from Altruistic Motives"—Abbott, 1963, 361). It seems clear that those questions (which are ultimately questions of practical judgment) need to be dealt with, but it is also clear, I think, that they are not the questions that Kant is concerned with in the Analytic of the second Critique.

Similarly, I think we can now see the inadequacy of that reading that interprets the argument of the Analytic as being primarily concerned with establishing the moral law. Aside from the fact that this interpretation could at best account only for Chapter 1 and that, moreover, it contradicts Kant's own claim that the moral law is a fact of pure practical reason, this interpretation inevitably biases us in the direction of reading the argument as being concerned solely with *pure* practical reason rather than with practical reason as such. It thus leads us *away* from an understanding of the argument's concern with empirically conditioned willing (and, incidentally, makes it even more difficult to understand how immoral willing is possible—a problem that is already difficult enough and that must eventually be dealt with).

Instead of either of these aims, the argument (according to our interpretation) is concerned with showing that there is a practical viewpoint that is distinct from the theoretical viewpoint but that does not contradict that viewpoint; and it is concerned with showing how such a viewpoint is possible. This aim actually has priority over those aims, because it is only with respect to the possibility of a practical viewpoint that a transcendental argument can be given concerning laws or objects for the will.

This aim also has broader implications for transcendental philosophy: It opens up a new cognitive realm, within which questions of valuation can be raised in a really meaningful way—that is, without reducing them to questions of mere mechanistic determination. And this is made possible by the fact that the human intellect, which in theoretical cognition is always dependent upon sensibility to provide its concepts with a content (without which they are empty and mere thoughts), in practical cognition actually produces its own object—instead of being determined by sensibility, practical reason determines our causal faculty immediately and through it determines sensibility. But our intellect remains, nevertheless, discursive: It does produce its own object, but it does not produce its object, so to speak, on its own territory—the object it produces is not an intellectual object but rather a will-determination. Practical reason's object (unlike the object of an intellectus archetypus) stands apart from itself in the world of fact (and that is true even if practical reason succeeds only so far as to determine the will, without actually producing an action). This is reflected in Kant's insistence that the moral law is synthetic: It combines in one will a pure law of reason and a determination of the will (neither of which can be derived analytically from the other).

So in the realm of practical reason we have a situation that is unique in transcendental philosophy: The human intellect, whose unity-functions are otherwise always in need of determination by a manifold that must be given, in this case itself determines a manifold; and yet it does so without ceasing to be discursive. This result of the practical philosophy would seem to have many implications for our understanding of the finitude of the human intellect. We cannot explore these implications here, but the question deserves further consideration.

Perhaps most remarkable of all is the fact that this new realm is opened up for transcendental philosophy by using (in addition to the sole Fact of pure practical reason) only those rational functions that belong to reason as such (i. e., regardless of whether reason is used for a theoretical or practical purpose)—namely, the analysis and synthesis of concepts. But this point leads us into consideration of more general conclusions that we can draw about transcendental arguments as such, which we will take up next.

Transcendental Arguments

In addition to providing an account of the aims and structure of the second Critique, I think the argument of the preceding chapters contributes to our understanding of Kant's transcendental arguments. The basic features of a transcendental argument that we outlined in Chapter 2 were developed on the hypothesis that the discursive character of our intellect and its relation to sensibility is of central importance to the transcendental form of argument. The subsequent substantiation of that model in our Chapters 4—7, therefore, gives strong support to our original hypothesis.

What we discovered in applying our model to the second Critique was that we could understand the problems that the argument was concerned with only by making reference to the faculties involved: In Chapter 1 of the Analytic, especially in the deduction, the argument was concerned with an a priori relation between reason and the will; in Chapter 2 the problem was one of practical understanding; and in Chapter 3 it was sensibility that had to be considered.

And not only the subject matter of the argument but the form of the argument itself was determined by the nature of our faculties: Because the intellect is finite we can never guarantee by concept analysis alone that a given concept is thought with all its essential determinations.

Concepts always stand in need of determination—they refer beyond themselves to their content. It was for that reason that our model of a transcendental argument included the must/can structure—which is an essentially synthetic form of argument; and that structure was found not only in the individual steps but in the Analytic as a whole.

So in the current debate over the nature of transcendental arguments we would, on the basis of our findings, have to side with those (like Hintikka, 1972) who maintain that Kant's so-called "psychological" assumptions are fundamental to his transcendental arguments; and we would have to side against those (like Gram, 1971, 1973, 1974; Körner, 1966, 1967; and Wilkerson, 1970) who claim that we can understand Kant's transcendental arguments in complete abstraction from those presuppositions.

That is not to say, of course, that the enterprise of generalizing the notion of transcendental arguments is a fruitless one. On the contrary, in a broad sense of the term "transcendental philosophy" we would want to be able to include such diverse thinkers as Husserl, Hediegger, Habermas, Strawson, and many others—none of whom would accept all of Kant's presuppositions about the nature of our finitude. But I do think that before we reject Kant's presuppositions we need to be quite clear (and quite precise) about what we are rejecting and what we are replacing it with; and that sort of clarity and precision are strikingly absent from most of the recent discussions of transcendental arguments (as is evidenced by the labeling of questions relating to the constitution of our faculties as "psychological apparatus"—cf. Wilkerson, 1970, 200).

I suspect that before we can make any really enlightening comparisons between Kant's transcendental arguments and more recent attempts at such arguments we need to understand Kant's arguments much more thoroughly. Our examination of the second Critique has already shown that certain of the features most commonly attributed to transcendental arguments as such need to be reformulated. For example, we now know that experience is not the only cognitive framework that can ground such an argument, since in the second Critique the argument is grounded by the practical viewpoint. We have also seen that the problem of a priori synthesis is not simply a problem of a priori predication but rather of the a priori relation of faculties. And we have seen that the unidirectional relation of determinability between intellect and sensibility is not a necessary feature of transcendental arguments.

But there are also important questions that we waived in our analysis of the second Critique and that need to be considered. For example, it would be important to be able to specify the role of deductions in transcendental arguments: Are they arguments complete in themselves, or are they only parts of a larger whole that they in some sense presuppose? And if the latter, how do they fit into the whole? I think our results point to the conclusion that a deduction in Kant's sense is only a part of a larger argument and that it cannot stand on its own. And it would also seem that the deduction in the second Critique, at least, does not differ from the rest of the argument with respect to its method but only with respect to its subject matter. But these suggestions are very tentative: They would have to be checked against the first Critique and other cases of deductions in Kant's works.

Also in the interest of greater precision, we need to be able to distinguish between different kinds of proofs and the different sorts of certainty they provide. In particular, Kant carefully distinguishes philosophical proofs from mathematical proofs, arguing that only in mathematics can a proof have absolute certainty. Philosophical proofs, on the contrary, are always subject to reexamination:

> Reason must not, therefore, in its transcendental endeavors, hasten forward with sanguine expectations, as though the path that it has traversed led directly to the goal, and as though the accepted premisses could be so securely relied upon that there can be no need of constantly returning to them and of considering whether we may not, perhaps, in the course of the inferences, discover defects that have been overlooked in principles, and that render it necessary either to determine these principles more fully or to change them entirely (KrV A735/B764 f.).

This points to a limitation of human reason that is more than simply our proneness to error: Kant's claim seems to be that there is an essential impossibility in the attempt to achieve absolute certainty in philosophical proofs (and that agrees with the considerations that led us to the must/can structure in transcendental arguments). I think that until we are clear on what to expect from a philosophical proof we can never be sure of our interpretation of Kant's arguments.

This last point seems particularly relevant in light of the attempt by some (e.g., Körner, 1966, 1967; Gram, 1971, 1973, 1974) to reduce the transcendental form of argument wholly to questions of formal logic. It is certainly reasonable to insist that any argument be logical, but it might nevertheless be the case that the questions peculiar to transcendental arguments simply cannot be posed in terms of logical implication alone. This, I take it, is the thrust of Crawford's argument (Crawford, 1963) and is her reason for developing the notion of framework questions. I think any treatment of this question would have to deal with Kant's distinction between formal and transcendental logic and explore the question of why that distinction is important and what it means for the proof in transcendental philosophy.

In any case, I think our examination of the second Critique has shown that it must be read as a transcendental argument and that, if we do so read it, we can make sense out of arguments that are otherwise unintelligible; and at the same time we have succeeded in a somewhat greater specification of the transcendental form of argument. These conclusions point to the need for further investigations, but at the same time they provide results that I think must be taken into consideration in any discussion of what a transcendental argument is.

APPENDIXES

The most complete English treatment of the second Critique is Lewis White Beck's *Commentary*; but that book does not deal to any significant degree with the topic that we are concerned with, namely, the argument-structure of the second Critique as transcendental argument. It is not even perfectly clear that Beck thinks the second Critique is really a part transcendental philosophy (cf. Beck 10, note and 262, note). But he does, nevertheless, interpret at least one section of the second Critique as a transcendental argument (namely, the section entitled "On the Deduction of the Principles of Pure Practical Reason"). Thus we can make twofold use of Beck's *Commentary*: in the first place, since it represents thorough and painstaking account of the entire book, but an account that for the most part does not consider the argument as a transcendent argument, we can use this account to show the limitations of such a treatment; and in the second place, since it does treat one part of the argument as a transcendental argument (and in the process makes use of the two most commonly referred to features of transcendental arguments—namely, the justification of a priori synthetic judgments and the establishment of the conditions of the possibility of experience), we can see how adequate such a approach is to the case of the second Critique. With these two aims in mind, I will first try to characterize Beck's overall approach to the second Critique and (at risk of doing injustice to his highly detailed work) to summarize his account of the argument-structure of the Analytic as a whole, and then I will present a more detailed account of his interpretation of chapter 1, Section 1 as transcendental deduction.

Beck at no point states what he thinks is to be proved in the Analytic a whole. Instead he names three problems: formulation of the law of pure practical reason, proof that pure reason can be practical through this law, and exposition of "those factors that make it possible that knowledge this law can in fact be a motive for action" (Beck 68). He never unites these problems under one general question (and thus he implicitly denies r claim that the Analytic represents a single—though complex—tran-

scendental argument). However, it is clear from the course of his commentary that he sees the central problem as being the establishment of
the moral law—so much so that he rearranges the sequence of the argument in order to present a transcendental deduction of that principle.
Since Beck sees the establishing of the moral law as being the central
problem, and since that problem would seem to be solved in Chapter 1,
he is led to interpret Chapters 2 and 3 as auxiliary to that central concern
Thus he sees Chapter 2 as part of a "metaphysical deduction" of the moral
law (i. e. , an exposition and formulation of the law—see Beck, 69—70):
Its purpose is to further clarify the moral law by introducing the specific
concepts used in judging according to that law (namely, the concepts of
good and evil). Thus Beck sees no problem peculiar to and solved in
Chapter 2. In a similar way, he interprets Chapter 3 as providing the
motive for the law: His argument is that the law alone cannot move a
person to action, so we need to establish a feeling to be the motive to
action (see Beck, 221—3).

If Beck's account of the general structure of the Analytic is right, then
it would seem that there really are no transcendental concerns in the
Analytic other than the deduction of the moral law. All the other argumen
of Chapters 2 and 3, would be concerned merely with deriving further
knowledge from the moral principle ("metaphysical" knowledge in the
sense in which Kant distinguishes it from transcendental knowledge in the
third Critique—KU, Introduction, Section V) or perhaps with contributing
to the firmer establishment of the moral law. In general, as we shall see
Beck does not distinguish a transcendental level of argumentation from
what we might call a psychologico-metaphysical level. One of our major
tasks, of course, is to distinguish more precisely between a transcendental form of argument and other similar forms that might seem to be concerned with the same questions. Beck's interpretations of the argument
in the second Critique are frequently colored by a tendency to look for
"mechanisms" of practical reason (he uses the word with reference to mc
feeling, for example—cf. Beck, 223 note 37) , which would imply that the

essential nature of the thing under consideration is known and all that is needed is a more complete   (mechanical) understanding of the way it functions. For example, his reading of the Typic sees it as providing a "schema" for use in practical judging rather than as solving a problem of the a priori determinability of a finite will by a pure practical law; and on his account Chapter 3 becomes more a metaphysical psychology than transcendental argument: Establishing a feeling as motive for morality is not a concern of transcendental philosophy, but rather of either psychology or the methodology of pure practical reason (and, indeed, Beck has difficulty distinguishing the aims of Chapter 3 and the Methodology—see Beck, 209—236). To see more clearly how Beck's approach to the argument affects his interpretation, we will have to examine more carefully his account of the progress of the argument in the Analytic.

Like every reader of the second Critique, Beck faces the extremely difficult problem of deciding, in the first place, what the realm of discourse of the book is. In particular, are we concerned with moral practical reason, empirically conditioned practical reason, or both? Kant calls his book a critique of practical reason, and in the Introduction he emphasizes that he is concerned with practical reason *in general*. Yet every chapter heading and subheading in the Analytic refers to the *pure* practical reason. This apparent confusion is reflected throughout the Analytic, appearing first at the very beginning of Chapter 1 and becoming most problematic with the introduction of the categories of freedom. Beck deals with the difficulty by arguing that Kant's real concern—primarily in the first chapter, but also in the Analytic as a whole—is to differentiate the pure use of practical reason from the empirically conditioned use and to establish the principles of the pure use (Beck, 66). Thus he interprets Kant's apparent jumping back and forth from one to the other as being a confusing attempt to distinguish the two (cf. Beck, 142—3).

This interpretation of Beck's is apparent in the arrangement of his commentary on Chapter 1. He reads Sections 1—3 and part of 8 as an analytic of empirical practical reason and sees Sections 4—7 and the other part of

8 as a "metaphysical deduction" of the moral law—i. e. , as an attempt to
show "what the law must be if the concept of duty and therewith all morality
are not spurious" (Beck, 110). Thereafter he sees the intrusion of elements
of the empirically conditioned will either as being part of Kant's attempt
to clearly distinguish the two or else as being for the sake of establishing
the moral law for a human (empirically conditioned) will. That turns out to
mean, as we shall see, that he is not able to read the book consistently as
a critique of practical reason in general.

Since Beck sees establishing the moral law as being the central concern
of the book, and since he believes that to mean that there must be a transcendental deduction of the law, he locates such a deduction in Section 7
and Part I (42—50) of Chapter 1. But he postpones that argument in his
commentary until after the discussion of Chapter 2, since he reads the
second chapter as contributing to the solution of his "Problem I"—the
formulation of the moral law (which should logically precede the deduction
of the law). In my discussion of Beck's interpretation I, in turn, will
postpone discussion of his account of the transcendental deduction and
first treat his accounts of Chapters 2 and 3.

Beck's reason for reading Chapter 2 as being part of the formulation of
the moral law is his belief that the exposition of the categories is primarily
for the sake of establishing categories of pure practical reason and sec-
ondarily for the sake of exhibiting a schema of the moral law. I think it
will become clear later that this approach forces a misreading of the
chapter; but since it does offer a certain plausibility (and since Kant's text
is confusing enough that we must be grateful for any attempted clarification) , we must take this account into consideration.

For our purposes we do not need to be concerned with the details of
Beck's commentary on Chapter 2 here: what is more important for us is
to make clear his understanding of what is being established in the chapter
and why it needs to be established. According to Beck Chapter 2 is concerned with the "elaboration and application of the formula" (the moral
law—Beck, 126). He thus divides the chapter into three parts: paragraphs

1—13, paragraphs 14—17, and the Typic; the first two parts he considers
"elaboration" and the third "application." Paragraphs 1—13 "define the
concepts of good and evil as the concepts of objects of practical reason"
(Beck, 129); paragraphs 14—17 develop the categories of practical reason;
and the Typic "prescribes the condition for the application of these concepts and principles" (Beck, 129). This is all in keeping with his claim
that the chapter is part of the formulation and clarification of the moral
law. His argument seems to be that since we have principles peculiar to
pure practical reason, there must also be concepts peculiar to pure practical reason, so our account of the mechanics of practical reason is not
complete until we have presented those concepts. Thus the only problem
Beck sees as being dealt with in the first two parts of the chapter is a
problem of the thoroughness of the exposition: We need a table of categories of pure practical reason because otherwise our task of a thorough exposition of the moral principle is not really complete.

The difficulty that Beck encounters in this interpretation is that the categories of freedom are in fact a table of categories not of *pure* practical
reason but rather of practical reason in general, and so, as they stand,
they do not serve the purpose of further elaboration and specification of
the moral law (on the contrary, from that point of view they would seem to
represent a step backwards, since they reintroduce the "confusion" between moral and nonmoral categories). Beck handles this difficulty by assuming that Kant was simply not clear in his exposition: What Kant should
have done was to first establish the categories of practical reason in general and then "introduce those of pure practical reason as a subclass"
(Beck 143). Apparently Beck interprets Kant's expression "categories of
practical reason in general (überhaupt)" in terms of set theory in such a
way that the moral categories taken together with the nonmoral ones com-
prise the entire set of categories of practical reason in general; I do not
think that that is what Kant means by the überhaupt, and I think we should
keep in mind the possibility that the categories of practical reason in general are something more than just the combination of moral and nonmoral
categories.[7] In any case, Beck is forced by his interpretation of the argument-structure to see some of the categories (originally every third cate-

gory, but then exception has to be made for the sixth and ninth categories, and the eleventh has to be added) as moral categories and the others as categories of empirically conditioned practical reason. As justification for reading the table as containing those two classes of categories he appeals to Kant's two statements—immediately before and immediately after the table—which explain how the categories are to be interpreted (namely, as categories of practical reason in general). Beck interprets "they proceed in order from those which are morally undetermined and sensuously conditioned to those which, being sensuously unconditioned, are determined merely by the moral law" (66) to mean that every third category should be a moral category. I will not now go into a detailed criticism of this interpretation; all that needs to be pointed out at this stage is that the categories in fact do not turn out to be arranged that way (as Beck in the end admits), and, moreover, that understanding of the arrangement is in direct conflict with Kant's claim that it is the categories of modality that "initiate the transition" to the principles of morality (67). As it turns out, the only feature of the table that would lead us to accept Beck's interpretation (and thus to see the table as a mixture of pure and empirical categories) is the presence of what looks like the moral law itself as the third category; without going into an alternative interpretation, I will simply suggest that the implication of the third category is that the *quantity* of a practical judgment alone does not give us the defining feature of a moral judgment. (That is, we need to give serious consideration to the possibility that the third category really is a category of practical reason in general rather than a category of morality.) In any case, Beck himself admits that on his account the table of categories fails in its (apparent) aim of further clarifying the the moral law, since it instead produces anew confusion between the pure and empirical uses of practical reason.

Beck then turns to the Typic. On his account the problem of the Typic is the problem of the application of the moral law: We know the moral law in the abstract, but in moral decisions we must be able to "bridge the con-

ceptual gap" between the pure law and concrete situations (Beck, 157).
Beck follows Kant's lead in presenting this problem as being analogous to
the problem of the Schematism in the first Critique. But Beck's interpretation of the problem is marred (as mentioned above) by his failure
to distinguish the psychological problem of application from a transcendental problem of application. This failure becomes most visible precisely when we look at the analogous problem in the first Critique: There
the problem is by no means "How do we use these categories of the pure
understanding in natural science?"—if that were the question it would
remain unanswered at the end of the chapter on the Schematism. The problem there is clearly a problem of transcendental philosophy. We are not
seeking a rule-of-thumb for concept application but are rather performing
a step in a transcendental argument establishing the objective validity of
pure concepts as applied to experience. What is needed is an a priori application of the concepts of the understanding to pure intuition in order to
ground the possibility of the application of pure concepts to intuitions in
experience (to appearances) (cf. A138/B177). Beck, however, apparently
reads the first Critique in a way similar to the way he reads the second,
since he says that the problem of the Schematism is to show "how the concepts are to be applied in experience, i.e., how occasions for the application of the categories are found and distinguished within experience"
(Beck, 127)—clearly a psychological problem rather than a problem of
transcendental philosophy. Thus, if the problem of the Typic really is
analogous to the problem of the Schematism, and if the problem really is
one of transcendental philosophy, then it must be not the problem of finding a guide for moral judging of given situations (a problem of methodology
and psychology) but rather of grounding the a priori applicability of the
moral law to practical experience. Beck never raises the problem in those
terms, and as a result, on his interpretation, the chapter on the Typic
seems to be mislocated in the book: There is no reason for it to occur
after the Table of Categories (since it is not they that are being
"schematized") except for the structural analogy with the first Critique.

The chapter on the incentives, Chapter 3, is in some ways the most difficult chapter in the second Critique, and its difficulty is largely due to the lack of clarity about what purpose it is intended to serve. The problem is a very real one, because Kant emphasizes repeatedly that the law determines the will directly, not by means of any feeling; thus if our aim in the second Critique is to establish the moral law, there seems to be no real need for any discussion of incentives: The law itself is the incentive to action—as was proved in Chapter 1—and that should be the end of the matter. Any further elaboration of how the law functions as incentive would seem to be extraneous to the central purpose of the book and would belong more to psychology than to a critique of practical reason. And yet, in fact, the Incentives takes up a sizable portion of the Analytic and presents us with what seems to be a superfluity of arguments (Beck calls the chapter "repetitious" and the "least well-organized chapter in the book"—Beck, 219). The first task, therefore, of any interpretation of Chapter 3 is to show why it is necessary to the argument of the Analytic at all.

According to Beck (and almost everyone else except Heidegger) the chapter on the incentives is necessary because we require a motive for the moral law. His argument is that the human will requires a feeling as incentive in order to act. The moral law itself cannot be the incentive ("In spite of what Kant says, the law *itself* is not the incentive. A law is just not the sort of thing that can be an incentive" Beck, 221), so we must supply a moral feeling. This feeling is not something that exists antecedently to the moral law, but rather is produced by the moral law itself. Thus on Beck's account the law is able to determine the human will to action only through the mediation of feeling: Feeling is the direct determining ground and the law a mediated determining ground. This interpretation would seem to be in direct contradiction to Kant's text; and it is paralleled by a mistake in Beck's translation of the crucial sentence in the second paragraph of Chapter 3 where Kant states the aims of the chapter: Beck tranposes the first clause of that paragraph, "Da man also ... zu verschaffen," from its original position, where it states what we must *not* do, to the place where Kant states what the aims of the chapter *are*. His translation reads: "For the purpose of giving the moral law influence on the will nothing remains but to determine carefully in what way the moral law becomes an incentive..." (72). [Abbott translates this passage more accurately as follows: "Since, then, for the purpose of giving the moral law influence over the will, we must not seek for any other motives that might enable us to dispense with the motive of the law itself, because that would produce mere hypocrisy, without consistency; and it is even *dangerous* to allow other motives (for instance, that of interest) even to cooperate *along with* the moral law; hence nothing is left to us..." Abbott, 164.] Beck's interpretation once again shifts the focus of the argument from concern with issues of a transcendental proof to concern with essentially psychological and methodological issues. And although he does see Chapter 3 as being concerned with a particular problem (rather than simply filling in details of exposition)—namely, the problem of supplying an incentive as motive power to moral action—that problem seems not to be the one that Kant intended the chapter to confront. Kant's statement of the aim of the chapter gives the problem as being to see in what way the moral law directly functions as an incentive for the human will; and unless we are content to read the chapter as an exposition of certain mechanisms in the human will (as empirical psychology), our task is to delineate a transcendental problem of the a priori relation of pure practical reason to the human faculty of desire in a practical framework. (Beck is aware of the fact that his interpretation of the aims of the chapter does not completely agree with the text—see Beck, 223, note 37.)

This completes our summary of Beck's "nontranscendental" interpretation of the argument-structure of the Analytic. We have seen two weaknesses of Beck's account: One is the tendency to transform philosophical arguments into psychological ones (and this is the immediate result of not viewing the argument as transcendental philosophy); and the other is the failure to see any integrating problem of the Analytic except the general

124   APPENDIX A: BECK

problem of justifying the moral law (which, by itself, is too vague a
problem to shed light on the argument-structure of the text). I think these
two difficulties mutually reinforce one another. If we approach the book
from the outset with the idea that it represents a part of transcendental
philosophy, then I think we can begin to see the issues it deals with as
problems peculiar to transcendental philosophy. And, on the other hand,
if we give up the idea that justification of the moral law is the central
concern of the Analytic and that it provides us with a means for understanding the structure of the argument, then we are left free to interpret
Chapters 2 and 3 in ways that are more consistent with the text.

Now we must look at Beck's account of the "transcendental deduction"
of the moral principle. The first and most obvious difficulty to be dealt
with is Kant's denial that the moral law either needs to be deduced or can
be deduced (47). Beck acknowledges Kant's claim, but he nevertheless
reads the section entitled "Of the Deduction of the Principles of Pure
Practical Reason" as being some sort of justification of the moral law[8]
(a reading that is to some extent justified: Kant does refer to the fact of
the moral law's being a principle of deduction of the positive concept of
freedom as itself providing a "credential" for the moral law). But if the
section is to be read as justification of the moral law or moral principle
(Beck seems to use the two terms interchangeably), then we need to know
exactly what sort of thing it is that we are justifying and what we will
accept as a justification of it. When Beck argues that the purpose of this
section is to justify the moral law, he seems to treat the moral law as
though it were a theoretical proposition. There are two problems with that
approach: One is that the justification of a proposition is not the same
thing as a justification of an act of judging (and it is the latter that is
Kant's concern in the deduction of the first Critique) — if we are to concern
ourselves with the synthesis in an act of judging then we have to consider
what is the nature of the things being synthesized, what difficulties
might prevent their synthesis, and how the synthesis can be justified a
priori; if we are concerned with the judgment simply as a given

proposition then we are interested primarily in the content of the judgment. The other problem with Beck's approach is that it does not consider whether there might not be a difference between the problem of judging for the purpose of theoretical knowledge and the problem of judging for the purpose of practical knowledge (that is, for the purpose of determining the will). As Kant presents it in Section 7, the fundamental principle is not a declarative proposition but rather an imperative—that is, it claims to incorporate a determination of the will, and we might reasonably expect this will-determination itself to be the subject of a practical deduction (but we would then have to distinguish such a deduction from moral didactics, whose aim would be to *instill* such a determination of the will). Beck does not explicitly deal with either of these problems, and, from the point of view of our inquiry, that leaves some crucial questions unanswered.

A second feature of Beck's approach that should be noted is that, although he refers us to the first Critique for our model of a transcendental deduction, he does not really concern himself with the argument in that chapter of the first Critique entitled the Deduction. Rather, he refers us to an argument in the Aesthetic (recapitulated at A87/B120—1), which Kant does call a "transcendental deduction of the concepts of space and time", and to another argument in the Principles, which Kant does not actually call a transcendental deduction (Beck, 170—1). Beck at one point does refer explicitly to the "deduction of the categories" in the first Critique, but his summary of the "abstract structure" of the argument at that point (Beck 172—3) is so abstract that the specific problem of the Deduction is lost. His aim seems to be to present the form of a transcendental deduction in such extremely general terms that we can altogether abstract from the specific forms of argument-structures in the first Critique. How successful that approach is in dealing with our problem will be seen on closer examination.

Beck's first statement of the general structure of a transcendental deduction is as follows: "It is a process of taking some body of alleged fact (e.g., mathematics or science) which has been challenged and showing (a) what its necessary presuppositions are and (b) what the consequences of denying these presuppositions are" (Beck 170). To flesh that out further we can refer to what Beck says we would expect in the second Critique following that scheme: "We should expect [Kant] to introduce here a notion very prevalent now, that of 'moral experience' as a realm to be analyzed, articulated, and established. A critical regression upon its presuppositions would lead him to one or more synthetic a priori propositions Their justification would not lie in a claim that they are 'firmly established in themselves' but by proof that they are principles without which the experience in question, as the prius, would be unintelligible" (Beck, 171–2). Here we see employed the two touchstones of transcendental argumentation: justification of a priori synthetic judgments (the moral principle) and a grounding of and by experience ("moral experience"). Since those features do seem to be the most obvious starting points for a deduction in practical philosophy, we should examine them more carefully.

If the deduction is concerned with an a priori synthetic judgment, and if—following Beck—we interpret "judgment" to mean "proposition" rather than "act of judging", then the first question is: What judgment is it concerned with? Beck usually speaks as though what needs justifying is the moral law or the moral principle (see for example Beck 174–5). But when it comes to stating that principle as a proposition he refers us back to the *Grundlegung*, where Kant talks about the proposition "A good will has as its maxims only universal laws" (Beck 173; cf. GMM 447). (Beck does not discuss the differences between this proposition and the fundamental principle.) There Kant says that the proposition is synthetic since by mere analysis of the subject, "a good will", we cannot arrive at the property of its maxims having as their content themselves considered as universal laws.

If the proposition were analytic the predicate would already be thought in the subject so that no external justification of the judgment would be needed. But in a synthetic judgment a predicate is linked to a subject in which it is not already thought, so that if the judgment is to be justified some independent evidence must be adduced which shows the subject and predicate to be in fact united. If the judgment were an a posteriori one, the independent evidence would be experience: The predicate would be shown to be linked to the subject in actual fact. If the judgment is a priori, as this one is, the union of subject and predicate is thought as being necessary, and since necessity cannot be supplied by experience, some other mode of justification of such judgments must be found.

In the theoretical realm it turns out that even though a priori synthetic judgments cannot be justified by appeals to experience, experience is not irrelevant to their justification: Insofar as we are concerned with establishing the objective validity of those a priori synthetic judgments, the question of their applicability to experience is always crucial to their grounding. To say that an a priori synthetic judgment is applicable to experience means that we can in fact find the synthesis which the judgment expresses exhibited in our experience. If the judgment in question is "All alteration must take place in accordance with the laws of cause and effect," we certainly could not justify it solely on the grounds of experience—in that case it would be a merely empirical judgment. Nevertheless, the fact that we do have coherent experience (rather than a mere "rhapsody" of sensations), which exhibits, among other things, cause and effect relationships, is essential to the grounding of that judgment. In the theoretical realm, at least, the argument is that the very existence of such a body of experience presupposes an a priori synthesis of pure intuitions under concepts; thus the fact of there being such experience (rather than the particular experiences) is part of the grounding of the argument. (The other part of the grounding is supplied by the a priori synthetic judgments and the arguments supporting them. Kant refers to this "double grounding" of transcendental arguments at A736—8/B764—6.)

Beck argues that in addition to experience (empirical intuitive knowledge), the deduction of theoretical synthetic a priori judgments requires a pure intuition, which serves a function like that of experience but without the contingency of experience. He describes the course of the deduction of the categories as being based on "holding concepts up to intuitions" (Beck, 173)—that is, the model for the deduction, on this account, would be empirical verification; but since the intuition cannot be empirical if the relation between concept and intuition is to be necessary, the argument must proceed by eliminating the empirical element to arrive at pure intuition. Pure intuition has the virtues of experience in that it can present us with intuitions united under concepts, and it can present them as "facts"; but it has the further advantage of not being contingent—the "facts" constructed in pure intuition are necessary and universal.

If we examine the deduction in the second Critique looking for these features, we would in the first place expect "moral experience" to provide part of the grounding of the argument; and we would also expect to be able to derive some sort of pure intuition to ground that moral experience— that is, some sort of pure determination of the "practical intuition" (the faculty of desire) by practical concepts or principles. Now it could well be argued that something like that does occur in the second Critique (and, in fact, Silber makes such a claim—see Appendix B), though it does not seem to occur in the chapter on the Deduction. The "fact" of pure practical reason could be interpreted as an "experience" of the faculty of desire being affected by practical reason, and that "experience" could then be developed as being based on an a priori determination of the faculty of desire (a "pure formal desire" analogous to the pure formal intuition). But Beck rejects that approach and instead develops an argument in which the role of pure intuition is played by the idea of freedom.

At the same time, Beck acknowledges that it is freedom that is the real demonstrandum of the deduction, although he still reads the deduction as establishing the moral law (or, rather, as establishing the proposition quoted above about the good will). He thus holds that the argument of the

deduction has the same form as his summary of the deductions in the first
Critique, with the moral principle occupying the place of the demonstrandum (even though it is not deduced) and freedom taking the place of intuition (even though what the argument actually does deduce is freedom) —
a version of the argument that Beck admits is rather "circuitous"
Beck, 175).

Thus on Beck's account the transcendental deduction consists in showing
that the positive concept of freedom is the condition of the possibility of the
moral law (just as pure formal intuitions of space and time are the condition of the possibility of mathematics), so that freedom can be deduced
from the law considered as fact. But since freedom already has at least
negative support from theoretical reason, and was in fact required by it,
the moral law in turn receives a "credential." As Beck puts it, "The fundamental law ... is not left a naked and isolated assertion or an assertion
surrounded by a closed, circular, and empty system" (Beck, 175).

There are a number of difficulties with this account of the argument-
structure of the Deduction. For one thing, Beck's summary of the general
form of a transcendental deduction is far too general to tell us anything
about the actual procedure of such an argument. In any case, his summary
of the form of a transcendental deduction seems to be reducible to the claim
that a transcendental deduction is an argument concerned with establishing
the conditions of possibility of some a priori synthetic judgment, and that
formulation does not shed any new light on the actual procedure of such a
deduction (as is indicated by the fact that it does not allow Beck to consider
the specific problem of the theoretical Deduction at all).

I think the major difficulty with Beck's account of this chapter is that he
insists upon seeing in it a justification of the moral law. I think the reason
Beck reads the argument that way is that he expects to find the justification
on a priori synthetic proposition (following the traditional account of
transcendental deductions). To question that interpretation, however, is not
suggest that a transcendental deduction does *not* have as its purpose the
justification of an a priori synthesis, but rather to suggest that we need to

understand that "a priori synthesis" in somewhat different terms. In the Deduction in the first Critique, what is justified is not particular principles, nor even particular categories, but rather the possibility, in general, of the synthesis of a manifold of sensibly given intuition under a pure concept in a single act of judgment—that is, "the universally possible employment in experience of the pure concepts of the understanding" (B159). And the justication of this "employment" of concepts is for the sake of showing how our representations can relate to objects that are not produced but given. Now, since in the practical realm objects are not given and we are not concerned with knowing objects theoretically, it should be clear that the central question of the practical deduction cannot be the *same* as that of the theoretical deduction. In order to be able to see both the similarities and the differences in the two deductions, we need to explore in much greater detail the whole question of a practical synthesis. For example, are we still concerned with the relation to the object? Is it the will's relation to objects that is in question? And assuming that that is at least a major part of our concern, then what *is* an object of practical reason, and what does it mean to say, for instance, that "we produce the object"? I think it is in this area that the real problem of the practical synthesis lies; and even though these questions do not readily fit the rubric of justifying a priori synthetic propositions, I think they do parallel the central question of the theoretical deduction in important respects. But Beck, by abstracting so completely from the actual problem of the Deduction in the first Critique, in his search for the "abstract structure" of the deduction, is prevented from seeing any demonstrandum except the moral law.

It is actually not even the moral law that is deduced according to Beck but rather Beck's restatement of the a priori synthetic proposition from *Grundlegung* that he cites. And I think the fact that Beck is able to replace the fundamental principle with another, different formulation is directly related to the difficulty mentioned at the outset, namely, that in the first place we need a greater clarification of what justifying the moral law even means. Under the covering phrase "justification of the moral law" there ies a whole complex of distinct but interrelated questions: For whom are ve justifying the law? If for God (for an absolutely pure practical reason) hen presumably it is sufficient to prove the objective validity of the roposition "An absolutely good will is one whose maxim can always have is its content itself considered as a universal law." But if we must justify he law for humans (for a finite rational will) then surely we would be required o demonstrate the necessary obligation of the law—that is, we would have o show the necessary relation of that law to a will which is also a faculty f desire. But nothing of that sort is demonstrated (or attempted) in Kant's hapter on the Deduction. Nevertheless, that does not mean that we are ustified in ignoring the specific nature of the human will (as opposed to he absolutely good will). What we need greater clarification on is the ques- ion of what we expect from a critique of practical reason *in general*.

We also need a method of argumentation in the practical realm that takes nto account the fact that we are dealing with a finite will but that is distinct rom moral didactics: Practical transcendental philosophy cannot have as :s aim moral exhortation, but rather the laying bare of the original pre- isposition in the human will to recognize the moral law. And the method ust also be distinct from empirical psychology—we are concerned with a riori determinations of the will that make possible empirical will-deter- inations. Thus the purpose of a critique of practical reason is in a sense theoretical one—that is, we are concerned with making intelligible a high- y problematic phenomenon, namely, the human will. It is true that our ltimate aim in this undertaking is to promote practical ends, but our im- iediate task is to provide insight rather than moral conviction. It is for at reason, I think, that Kant repeatedly emphasizes that we cannot (and o not need to) justify the moral law. The moral law, as recognized by the uman will in the experience of moral obligation, establishes a practical iewpoint that needs to be investigated. Our task is to make that viewpoint telligible rather than to justify the fundamental law of the practical realm. 'hus our interests require us to go beyond Beck's concerns and reexamine the question of what a transcendental argument would require in the practical realm.

If, instead of looking for the "vainly sought deduction" of the moral law, we look for the more general problem of the practical synthesis, we will discover, I think, that the positive concept of freedom poses an equally important problem of a priori synthesis, namely, the synthetic relationship between a rational, unconditioned cause and its conditioned effects in nature [freedom as "causality of pure reason" (48) "which can be regarded as a faculty directly determining the will" (46)]. In that case Kant's claim that freedom (in the positive sense) is the demonstrandum would be justified.

This interpretation of the purpose of the Deduction, besides agreeing with Kant's own statements about the section, allows us to see an intellgible progress in the argument. On Beck's account the Deduction would really be only a repetition of the argument of Section 6, nor would it lead naturally into Chapter 2. But if we really accept Kant's claim that the central concern is to deduce the positive concept of freedom (and for a practical reason in general, not just for a pure practical reason), then we can see the Deduction as breaking new ground (namely, the interpretation of the positive concept of freedom as unconditioned causality of a sensibly conditioned will) and as introducing the problem of how we are to understand the unity of a will which, as pure reason, does not require objects as determining grounds, but which, as finite, necessarily represents to itself objects as conditions of its determination. And that, in turn leads directly into the problem of Chapter 2, which is to show how, from a practical viewpoint, the concepts of objects of practical reason in general are necessarily limited by the fundamental principle of pure practical reason.

Now, Beck by no means ignores the problem of freedom; on the contrary he devotes an entire chapter to the topic. And in that chapter he very insightfully reveals the complex nature of the positive concept of freedom. But since it is not his intention to exhibit the structure of the Analytic as transcendental argument, his treatment of freedom draws upon reference from different parts of the book rather than emphasizing their relation to their place in the argument.

The examination of Beck's treatment of the over-all argument-structure has shown us those specific aspects of the Analytic that pose the most difficulties for interpretation (the problem of interpreting the categories of freedom as categories of practical reason in general, the problem of reading the Typic as transcendental philosophy rather than as metaphysics of morals or psychology, and the problem of integrating Chapter 3 with the argument); and I have tried to suggest how those difficulties are related to reading the argument as dogmatic rather than transcendental. We now see similar problems in Beck's treatment of the "transcendental deduction," but here the problem seems to be, on the one hand, that Beck expects to find a deduction of the moral law (which Kant denies) and, on the other hand, that he does not devote enough attention to the transcendental problem of the practical deduction (or to transcendental deductions in general). We are left with the task of showing how the deduction and elaboration of the positive concept of freedom is necessary to the argument, and (more generally) of clarifying the transcendental form of argument.

Scattered through John Silber's many articles on Kant's moral philosophy we can find the pieces of a fairly systematic account of the argument-
structure of the second Critique. His account focuses on the importance
for the argument-structure of the object of practical reason, and at the
same time he insists that the moral philosophy must be read as transcendental philosophy.

Moral Philosophy as Transcendental Philosophy

Silber's contribution to the understanding of practical philosophy as
transcendental philosophy is that he insists upon the need for a realm of
"moral experience" to ground the arguments (Silber, 1960, cii; cf. Silber,
1959c, 204, 317). If we could establish the existence of such a realm we
could argue that freedom (or possibly the moral law) was a condition of its
possibility, and we would thereby have a basis for reading the argument
as transcendental in the sense in which Kant explicates the term in the
first Critique (e.g., KrV A736/B764 f.) as depending upon the possibility
of experience. (Beck mentions this possible tack but immediately dismisses
it—Beck, 1966, 171.) But Kant explicitly denies the possibility of such a
proof at the outset of the Deduction in the second Critique (46—47). His rea
son is precisely that neither freedom nor the moral law can ever be exhibited in experience (47).

Silber interprets Kant's denial as meaning that Kant intends to limit the
realm of morality to the noumenal realm (Silber, 1960, cii). Silber rejects
that position on the grounds that the Fact of pure practical reason (by which
he understands our awareness of moral obligation), which is the fundamental moral "experience," must occur at some time and therefore deserves
to be called experience in the full sense (empirical knowledge—knowledge
in which concepts are united with empirical intuition—cf. 42). This would
of course mean, as Silber recognizes, that there are elements in our experience to which the categories do not apply (*ibid.*); but that would imply

a reassessment of the results of the first Critique whose full gravity I think Silber does not recognize.

This difficulty with introducing peculiarly moral events into our experience arises not only with the so-called Fact, but with any experience understood as violating the laws of nature. Nor does it matter, for the solution of this problem, what we understand by the Fact. Silber identifies the Fact as an awareness of moral obligation. Beck has a rather complicated analysis which would interpret "the fact of pure practical reason" as meaning "the fact *that there is* a pure practical reason" (Beck, 1966, 166–7). Kant, at different places seems to mean by the Fact the moral law, freedom, our awareness of obligation, and our awareness of an a priori determination of our will (and I think ultimately we must be able to see how the Fact involves all of these aspects rather than identifying it with one). But no matter how we identify the Fact, if we insist that it is experienced but is not explicable by natural laws then we have undermined the foundations of theoretical knowledge.

Silber's position, nevertheless, has several virtues: It would allow us to construct an argument having a foundation in the possibility of experience; and even more importantly it would allow us to include sensible elements in our account of the argument, since the concept of experience includes both a rational and a sensible component. It is this latter point that is significant for Silber, since it is precisely the will's relation to objects (as capable of being presented in intuition) that he is concerned with. And it is important for us, in the first place, because we must be able to read the argument as ultimately treating not just a rational will, but a human will, which means a sensibly conditioned will; and, in the second place, because it would provide a way to understand the factuality of the Fact.

But the undermining of the results of the first Critique seems too high a price to pay for these advantages (valuable though they would be for our task). I have therefore outlined (Appendix C: The Fact) an alternative interpretation that takes into account the problems Silber points out (plus other problems raised in the first and third Critiques) and yet allow us to avoid the undesirable consequences of redefining "experience" to include events not subject to the categories of the understanding.

Silber, however, holds that we can be aware of ourselves as moral agents and that that awareness (which he calls experience) reveals a realm that needs to be explored and grounded. He bases his interpretation of the argument-structure of the second Critique on this realm and the attempt to establish the conditions of its possibility.

The Argument-Structure

The Categorical Imperative

Silber is interesting to us primarily because his account of the argument structure of the second Critique sees the argument as centered on the concept of an object of practical reason; but he also, briefly, explores the problem of deducing the moral law (he frames the question to be answered as "How is the categorical imperative possible?"—Silber, 1966, lxxxii). Silber's exploration of the problem and its attempted solution is not closely tied to the text of the second Critique (in fact, he holds that although the second Critique tries to answer the question it fails to do so—cf. Silber, 1966, lxxxiii), focusing instead primarily on the *Religion*; and I will not go into it in detail here. But his attempt is important since it represents one tempting approach to understanding what it would mean to deduce the moral law—namely, the approach that assumes that to deduce the moral law means to show (in a very strong sense) *why* we must obey it. Silber holds that Kant tried to prove that "reason supplies the power of freedom" (Silber, 1966, cxxx), so that to reject the laws of reason is to relapse into impotence. If such an argument were valid it would, of course, be very powerful, but its flaws are so obvious that they hardly need to be spelled out. (Briefly, I think this approach ultimately requires making the moral law the *ratio essendi* of freedom rather than the other way around. In general, any argument aimed at establishing the moral law must not do so at the expense of proving the impossibility of actions not determined by the moral law.)

The Highest Good

Silber argues that the second Critique can be read as a continuous argument establishing the highest good as object of practical reason (see especially Silber, 1962–63, 184; also Silber, 1959a, 469; Silber, 1959b, 99; Silber, 1959c, 202). The motivating force of the argument seems to be that, without an object, moral experience would be impossible. The problem, as he presents it, seems to be essentially the problem raised by the so-called Hegelian criticism of Kant's moral philosophy, namely, that the moral law, being a purely formal law, is empty and can have no material content. Silber maintains that a major purpose of the second Critique is precisely to "provide material content" for the moral law (Silber, 1962–63, 195; cf. 183, 191, 197 n41) in the form of an object, the highest good, and thus to ground moral experience from the side of sensibility.

He sees Chapter 1 as proving (on the basis of the possibility of our experience of obligation) that the concept of the good must be derived from the moral law rather than the other way around. According to his account, Chapter 2 is concerned with "determining an object for the will by means of the law itself"—namely, the good (Silber, 1962–63, 184); the Typic then provides a "sensible interpretation" of the object (*ibid.*)—that is, it shows that the concepts of good and evil "can determine definite sensible objects for the will" (*ibid.*). He then reads Chapter 3 as rescuing the self-determination of the will from any apparent encroachments by the material object supplied in Chapter 2.

Since Silber does not claim that this account of the argument-structure is exhaustive, it is not fair to tax him with omissions. Still, it is worth noting that this account neglects the Deduction and the Table of Categories. It also, I think, misdirects our attention in significant ways: In Chapter 2, by seeking a "sensible interpretation," it encourages us to look for a link between the moral law and sensibility (a Schematism); but the point of the chapter, and especially of the Typic, is to deny that such a link can be given and to argue that what is needed in the first place is a link with the understanding as faculty of concepts (since the moral law is grounded not in the understanding but in reason). This misemphasis, in turn, causes us to neglect the fact that the link with sensibility *is* discussed, but in Chapter 3 rather than Chapter 2; and the discussion there is not just an afterthought to the preceding chapters: Its task is to make intelligible the a priori feeling of respect, which is a necesary component of the Fact upon which the argument is grounded.

Rather than discuss Silber's account of the argument-structure step by step, I will try to show that a reading of the argument that sees it as primarily concerned with providing an object for the law must first clarify what it means to be an object of practical reason and to be the material content of the moral law. Only then will it become clear why, for example the argument must deal first with the practical understanding and only afterwards with practical sensibility (rather than having the steps Silber outlines); and only then can the question of *what* the object is be fruitfully raised.

We would expect the topic of the object of practical reason to be discussed under the concept of an end. The human will is a finite practical understanding, and as such it is a faculty of desire. The faculty of desire, according to its transcendental defintion, is "the faculty a [living] being has of causing, through its ideas, the reality of the objects of these ideas' (9 n7). An end, according to its transcendental definition, is "the object of a concept so far as this concept is regarded as the cause of the object (the real ground of its possibility)" (KU Section 10). Thus the human will can be thought of as a "faculty of ends" (58—9). It is determinable by the conception—according to rules—of an object as possible effect of its causality.

But of course the will is also determinable by the moral law, and this mode of determination turns out to be radically different from determination by ends. It is a central tenet of the second Critique that the determination of the pure will by the moral law does not require the representation of an object—in fact, if it were determined in that way it would not be morally determined, since that kind of determination can occur only through a feeling of pleasure or pain, which is always empirically condi-

tioned and contingent. Rather than first presenting the will with an object,
the moral law determines the will directly; the subsequent determination
of an object is a separate function of the moral will-determination:

> [Philosophers] should have looked for a law that directly
> determined the will and that only then determined the object
> suitable to it (64).

(Beck's translation of this sentence is misleading: he makes the philosophers the subject of "determine" rather than the law.) Thus a discussion of
the object of practical reason under the concept of an end would have pre-
judiced the question of whether the faculty of desire could be determined
in ways other than by pleasure.

Another way of seeing how fundamental is the difference between the
moral object and the natural object is to ask the question What is it that
is judged in the moral law? It is certainly not physical objects, nor actions—it is not an end nor a means to an end—nor ultimately is it even the
maxims of actions; rather, it is the *subject*: "the acting person
himself as a good or evil man" (60). What the law commands us to will is
ourselves as moral persons. Thus the moral law does not have, in the first
place, an object but rather a subject (cf. 87—88, 131).

At the heart of this difference is the human understanding and its
"peculiarity," namely, that it is discursive. The human understanding is
finite; in its theoretical employment that means that—unlike an intellectual intuition—it does not give itself its own objects (strictly speaking, an
intellectual intuition would not even have objects in the way a discursive
intellect does). Instead it functions through concepts, which are only rules
for synthesis of a manifold that must be given from elsewhere. In its practical employment the understanding is still discursive: As a finite will,
whose satisfaction necessarily requires reference to objects which must
be given, it wills the unity of a manifold of desires in general under "the
unity of a practical reason commanding in the moral law, i.e., of a pure
will" (65). The practical understanding, then, has a reference to the unity
of consciousness—practical reason—and also to a sensible manifold—

feeling. Both reason and sense provide grounds of its determination: reason immediately, in the moral law, and sense mediately, through the representation of an object as desirable. The fact that practical understanding is necessarily concerned with the existence of an object links it with sensibility (pleasure/pain). To the extent that pleasure/pain is incorporated into its determination it functions as a faculty of ends. But since feeling is not the only ground of its determination it is not restricted to being determined by desires (i.e., under the concept of objects as ends). As determinable directly by the moral law the practical understanding (in willing its maxims as united in a ground not given in sense) has no object but itself as moral, i.e., as grounding its maxims in the pure law of practical reason. (This is a strong conclusion that can be drawn from the fact that the moral law is a law for *all* rational beings, not just those with discursive wills.) But even when determined by the moral law, in willing a unity of its maxims practical understanding can have as its content only the subject represented under the practical concept of an object in general (an end in general), so that the subject would be willed in a sense as an end, but as a pure unconditioned end. The subject-as-moral is an end whose attainment does not depend upon conditions of external givenness but is produced solely by a self-activity, so that this concept of end serves as the limiting condition of all ends. (It is along these lines that we can begin to distinguish the concept of an end-in-itself from the concept of an ultimate or final end.) The will determined by the moral law would be analogous to an intellectus archetypus, creating its object (this is a radical sense in which the will can be the "cause of its object"—cf. 66 although even in this case the matter of the will is still distinct from its form). Thus the pure will-determination would be in its very essence an awareness of a self-determination and to that extent self-awareness (though it involves awareness of the subject only as pure causal object in general—that is, awareness of the unity of the pure will in its willing).

To the extent that practical understanding is conditioned by feelings it is purely a faculty of desire. And the object of a faculty of desire must be represented as possibly existing in nature in order for it to be a determining ground of the will. Although the will in this sense can still be said to produce its object, it depends for its satisfaction upon feeling, which is a receptive faculty. Since it is determined in accordance with a representation of expected satisfaction, there is an intrinsic contingency in its functioning. Pleasure/pain is that aspect of empirical experience that presents the subject to itself as affected by an object. As such it has a reference to an object (since it is a mode of receptivity) but is not objective since it presents, in the first place, the subject (the empirical subject as affected by an object). Thus our understanding cannot represent its object (the end) as necessarily providing sufficient grounds of pleasure for its determination; it can only represent its own pleasure as a powerful but contingent ground of determination. (This feature is intimately linked to the fact that empirical feeling is experienced in inner sense and, as such, must always appear with a definite quantity and qualitative intensity.)

It turns out, then, that Kant's having abstracted from the relation to an object in arriving at the pure moral law must be interpreted in a more radical sense than as just having left the object out of consideration. The way pure practical reason relates to objects is radically different from the way will as faculty of desire relates to objects, so that virtue as an object of the will (the supreme good) is different *in kind* from happiness. The functioning of practical understanding is in both cases the same, but its content is different; in both cases it can be said to be related to an object, and even to an end, but in very different senses (the object of pure practical reason is originally a subject who is an end-in-itself; for virtue to become an end there must already be an a priori determination of the will by the moral law).

That means that the problem of uniting the two objects into a single object (which requires willing them both at one and the same time under the same maxim) is much more difficult than it might at first appear. To even approach this problem requires dealing with the features peculiar to the pure practical reason, practical understanding, and practical sensibility to seek out the conditions of the possibility of an a priori relationship among them. This line of reasoning, then, indicates that the division of the Analytic of the second Critique into chapters on principles, concepts, and incentives is not just a feature of the architectonic but results from the nature of the subject-matter.

Independent evidence for this interpretation (which makes clearer the necessity of viewing the problem as one of transcendental philosophy) is to be found in a footnote in the *Religion*. There Kant points out that "it is one of the inescapable limitations of man and his faculty of practical reason (a limitation, perhaps, of all other worldly beings as well) to have regard, in every action, to the consequence thereof, in order to discover therein what could serve him as an end ..." (Religion IX-XI). This necessity for an end requires, from the point of view of reason, an "extension" (to include possible objects of desire), which extension can only be justified by reference to "the a priori principle of the knowledge of the determining grounds of a free will in experience in general" (*ibid.* —I have altered Greene and Hudson's translation slightly). At the very least, this (extremely difficult) passage clearly indicates that the problem of an objec of practical reason is a transcendental one and requires an investigation of the features peculiar to the human will.

These considerations primarily concern the object of practical reason simply in its status as object of practical understanding—as end—not as having subjective material content (pleasure and pain). The problem of ma terial content is twofold since it can refer to the will's relation to an objec simply as an effect of free causality or to the will's relation to the subjec- tive grounds of the desire for that object, namely, feelings of pleasure an pain (cf. 16 and 75). An adequate account of material content must deal wi both of these. The former—the objective material content—is considered in Chapter 2. The second—the subjective material content—is what is con sidered in Chapter 3 (though only in relation to the particular problem of t

Critique, namely, the pure will's a priori relation to feeling). Thus I think Silber's approach tends to obscure the root problems of the Critique and the way they relate to an interpretation of the argument as transcendental argument.

A further danger of this approach is the interpretation it places on the will's "need" for a material object (which is the motive-power of Silber's argument). In his article on the practical schematism Silber argues that without material content the moral law is "leer und unfruchtbar" (Silber, 1966, 256). If that means that the moral law's ability to determine the will depends upon our ability to represent to ourselves a sensible object, then it is misleading. That interpretation turns the real problem upside-down by making it seem as though our task were to provide a part needed for the functioning of the moral machinery, whereas in fact that part is necessarily provided by practical understanding, and the real problem is to show how it can be united into the transcendental mechanism. It is not the case that our will could fail to have an object (and be made perplexed and impotent by the lack). Human practical understanding functions by setting itself objects (ends), so that even though the moral law determines the practical understanding immediately, our awareness of that determination always involves conceiving the subject and its virtue as objects and ends. And this feature of our will—that it always conceives its own determination in terms of ends—belongs to our will simply as *finite* rational will (as practical understanding), without regard to the mode of sensible conditioning.

Silber's focusing on the object of practical reason as thematic concern of the argument fills an important gap in Beck's account of the argument (which focused on the justification and elaboration of the moral law). And his insisting on the fundamental importance of the Fact (even though we must reject his interpretation of the Fact as experience) points the way both to a firmer grounding of the argument and to a deeper set of questions about our moral awareness. But if we are to follow Silber's lead and at the same time read the argument as transcendental argument grounded on the Fact, we need to raise the question of the object on all levels and not just on the level of the particular material content of a will-determination.

APPENDIX C: THE FACT OF PURE PRACTICAL REASON

The question of the nature of the Fact and its factuality is an extremely difficult one. To simplify it somewhat I will take for granted that the Fact is our awareness of the immediate determination of our will by the moral law (or, more simply, it is the awareness of moral obligation). I will therefore consider here only the following question: How can the Fact, without being a fact of experience, be factual?

Kant's assertions that the Fact is not a fact of experience are so clearly and strongly stated that it would seem that there could be no disagreement on that point:

> The moral law is given as an apodictically certain fact, as it were, of pure reason, a fact of which we are a priori conscious, even if it be granted that no example could be found in which it had been followed exactly. Thus the objective reality of the moral law can be proved through no deduction, through no exertion of the theoretical, speculative, or empirically supported reason; and even if we were willing to renounce its apodictic certainty, it could not be confirmed by any experience and thus be proved a posteriori. Nevertheless, it is firmly established of itself (47)

(cf. 31; 57; see also KU Section 91 on matters of fact). Nevertheless, there is a tendency in the literature to refer to the Fact as "moral experience"; Silber, for one, flatly rejects Kant's claim that the Fact is not a fact of experience, and his argument has a certain persuasivenes about it:

> The experience of moral obligation—which Kant called the fact of pure reason—occurs in time, in inner sense, and therefore involves sensible intuition (Silber, 1960, cii).

That is, to formulate an argument from this passage, our awareness of the determination of the will by the moral law must certainly occur at some time and therefore must be presented in intuition. But if it is presented in intuition then it must be experienced. Therefore the moral fact is a fact of experience.

But Kant's reasons for not admitting the moral Fact into experience are very good ones: To call the Fact an experience would be to overthrow the conclusions of the first Critique, since it would force us to admit into experience an instance of unconditioned causality.

To help us find our way out of these difficulties I propose the following:

The moral Fact is *not* an experience, although it contains elements that are also part of our experience (and it is these elements that provide the factuality of the Fact); but the moral Fact includes, in addition to those elements that are also part of our experience, another awareness that is not given in intuition but that is rather an immediate self-awareness of our own causal activity. This second element could be called a practical *apperception*, and I will cite passages from the first Critique and the *Groundwork* in which Kant refers to such an awareness.

First, however, we need to examine those elements of the Fact that also form parts of our experience. In becoming aware of the determination of our will by the moral law (for instance, through the example that Kant gives when he first introduces the Fact— 30), what gives the awareness the quality of factuality is that we know our will to be actually determined to act, and we know that through *feeling* the will-determination. What we feel is (to use Kant's terminology) our life-force being channeled in a certain direction. This feeling is, like all feeling, a product of sensibility, and so it presents the will-determination as phenomenon (and, consequently, it presents the will-determination as, indeed, occurring at some particular time). The complete description and explanation of the various elements of the feeling is the concern of empirical psychology. But, among other things, the feeling involves a determination of pleasure and pain. In particular, it involves those determinations of pleasure and pain that we are familiar with from our discussion of respect (Chapter 7 above).

Now, all of these features of the feeling through which the determination of the will by the moral law is announced are available to be taken up into our experience. In fact, they *must* be able to be incorporated into our experience precisely because they are given in inner sense, and there cannot be stray intuitional data that are incapable of being brought to the unity of consciousness under concepts (as was proved in the first Critique). In order to be incorporated into experience, a cause must be assigned to the will-determination, and that cause must itself be a sensible given that is either prior to or contemporaneous with the will-determination. That is, insofar as it is part of our experience, the moral will-determination will always appear within a causal sequence as the effect of some prior pheno-menal event. Since (by hypothesis) in moral determination of the will there is no preexisting desire that could appear as cause of the will-determina-tion, there is only the feeling of respect (or the associated feeling of self-approbation) that can appear as cause of the will determination. So insofar as we consult our experience of moral will-determination we will always find ourselves determined to the action by some feeling (namely, respect for the moral law, or perhaps the desire to be able to maintain our own self-respect). This is the inevitable result of the constitution of our facul-ties of *theoretical* cognition; it is an instance of a process to which Kant gives the name "transcendental subreption," which is the (inevitable) mis-take of assigning to our receptivity (or to the object represented through our receptivity) what really belongs to our spontaneous activity (cf. 176—7; KrV A402; A582/B610 f. ; A791/B819; KU, Section 27; and first Introduction to KU, Ak. 222). The ultimate reason for this inevitable subreption is that we can know ourselves (and our activities) only as phenomenal and there-fore as given; so we can only know our own spontaneous activity insofar as our sensibility is passively affected by it (at least, this is the case if we restrict the meaning of "knowledge" to theoretical knowledge).

In any case, the Fact does contain elements that, because they are data available to be incorporated into experience, are undeniably factual; but to the extent that those data *are* incorporated into experience they are as-signed not to their true source (pure reason) but rather to the phenomenal (sensibly conditioned) self. If we had no other awareness of our own activity than the effects that it produces on our sensibility then the moral Fact would be simply an impossibility, and even if we were free we could never know it.

But we do have another source of such awareness—namely, appercep-tion. We can have theoretical knowledge of ourselves only through experi-ence, but we can have a certain awareness of ourselves through appercep-tion. In the first Critique Kant argues that we are conscious of the "I think" not as knowledge (and therefore not as experience) but as a *thought* (KrV B157). This thought contains nothing but the consciousness of the

unity of the act in the synthesis of a manifold and is therefore the consciousness of myself as an object in general (and thus not self-consciousness
in any strong sense). Nevertheless, the "I think" is a representation to
myself of the "spontaneity of my thought" (KrV B158); and it is "owing to
this spontaneity that I entitle myself an intelligence" (*ibid.*).

At the end of the B-edition version of the Paralogisms, Kant alludes to
a possible practical apperception that would be *more* than a mere thought:

> Should it be granted that we may in due course discover, not in experi-
> ence but in certain laws of the pure employment of reason—laws that
> are not merely logical rules, but that while holding a priori also con-
> cern our existence—ground for regarding ourselves as *legislating*
> completely a priori in regard to our own *existence*, and as determin-
> ing this existence, there would thereby be revealed a spontaneity
> through which our reality would be determinable, independently of the
> conditions of empirical intuition. And we should also become aware
> that in the consciousness of our existence there is contained a some-
> thing a priori, which can serve to determine our existence—the com-
> plete determination of which is possible only in sensible terms—as
> being related, in respect of a certain inner faculty, to a nonsensible
> intelligible world (KrV B430 f.).

And in the solution to the third Antinomy he refers to this apperception as
knowledge (Erkenntnis):

> Man, however, who knows all the rest of nature solely through his
> senses, knows himself also through pure (blosse) apperception; and
> this, indeed, in acts and inner determinations which he cannot regard
> as impressions of the senses (KrV A546/B574).

Finally, in the *Groundwork* Kant also speaks of a "consciousness that
reason is independent of purely subjective determinations by causes that
collectively make up all that belongs to sensations" (GMM 457), and he
refers to "whatever there may be in man of pure activity (whatever comes
into consciousness not through affection of the senses, but immediately)"
(GMM 451).

I think the conclusion that must be drawn from these passages is that,
in addition to those elements of the Fact that we are aware of through
sense and that can be incorporated into experience, there are elements
that we are aware of through apperception and that are not experienced,

namely, the awareness of the spontaneous activity of reason in determining the will.

These, then, are the two (essentially distinct) elements that go to make up our awareness of the moral law. But there is one further point that needs to be made about these elements. Presumably they would be present in our awareness of *any* will-determination: A determination of our will will always be announced in sensibility. And the determination of our will always involves reason, so there should also always be an awareness of the spontaneity of reason in any awareness of a will-determination. What makes the moral Fact unique is that *pure* reason determines the will, and that must somehow be included in the awareness of the Fact both on the level of apperception and on the level of sensibility.

On the level of apperception it is easy enough to see how the purity of the rational will-determination is recognized: In Sections 1—7 of Chapter 1 Kant proves that the moral law is the only practical rule that carries with it necessity in the determination of the will—all other practical rules presuppose some empirical and therefore contingent content. So only in the case of determination of the will by the pure moral law can reason be aware of a determination that is practically *necessary*. (That does not, of course, mean that in every empirical instance of moral willing the thought of the moral law and its necessity will be present, but rather that the moral law and only the moral law can be shown, on a priori grounds, to supply a necessary determination of the will. The consciousness of necessity is therefore always available to practical apperception a priori, even though it may be absent in a given case of willing.)

On the level of sensibility the determination of the will by pure reason is announced in the peculiar quality of the moral feeling—namely, in its character of rejecting all inclinations as such as determining grounds of the will (see our Chapter 7). Respect, although it is itself a determination of the faculty of pleasure and pain, is like no other feeling, because it is made possible only by pure reason's ability to reject all inclinations as determining grounds and instead to determine the will immediately. Since respect is a feeling (and since it has associated with it the feeling of self-approbation) it is able to be incorporated into experience as the cause of the moral will-determination (through a subreption). But since it is a feeling produced by the rejection of all sensible determining grounds as such, it is like no other feeling and, in fact, reveals its origins in the determination of the will by pure reason.

If this account is essentially correct, We can see how the Fact of pure practical reason is both factual and nonexperiential: It contains data that are also (from a different viewpoint) data of experience, but those data—by virtue of their own characteristics and by virtue of the pure apperception that accompanies them—can and must be viewed also from a practical viewpoint as a pure practical fact.

APPENDIX D: MAXIMS AND LAWS

The distinction between maxims and laws is of great importance both for the argument of the Analytic (which begins with an Erklärung of the distinction) and for our understanding of Kant's transcendental philosophy. Discussion of this distinction will lead us into consideration of the most fundamental problems of the practical philosophy and will shed light on the aims and organization of the Analytic.

I propose orienting the discussion with respect to two questions: (1) How do maxims and laws differ? And (2) How can maxims be willed as laws? The first question is frequently answered by simply referring to Kant's criterion that maxims must be universalizable if they are to be willed as laws. From that it is concluded that the essential distinction is one of universalizability: If a maxim is universalizable then it is a law; if it is not, then it is a mere maxim. Beck, for example, holds this view, and he therefore (quite consistently) argues that Kant's terminological division is "logically faulty" since " 'maxim' is broader than 'law' and, in fact, includes 'law' as one of its species" (Beck, 1966, 81). From this point of view, then, the problem of maxims becoming laws (the second question) is really no problem at all—it is simply a matter of our always acting on maxims that are universalizable rather than on maxims that cannot be universalized without contradicting themselves. (I am leaving out of consideration the question of precisely what "universalizability" means and how it is decided.)

But I do not believe that Kant would be guilty of so elementary an error as that, and I also think that a distinction is involved that is more fundamental than the criterion of universalizability. So I propose the following theses: (1) Maxims and laws (although, viewed simply as propositions, they are both species of the genus "principle") are to be distinguished as functions of irreducibly distinct faculties, and as such they are themselves irreducibly distinct. Correspondingly, I claim that (2) moral willing (willing maxims as laws) involves two distinguishable (if not distinct) acts—one the willing of the maxim and the other the willing of the pure form of the maxim as a law (and these two acts are combined as the willing of the maxim *for the sake of* its pure lawful form). I will deal with these two theses consecutively.

Maxims versus Laws

In order to substantiate my claim about the essential difference of functions involved in maxims and laws we should look at Kant's own ways of distinguishing the two:

> A *maxim* is a subjective principle of action and must be distinguished from an *objective principle*—namely, a practical law. The former contains a practical rule determined by reason in accordance with the conditions of the subject (often his ignorance or again his inclindation). It is thus a principle on which the subject *acts*. A law, on the other hand, is an objective principle valid for every rational being; and it is a principle on which he *ought to act*—that is, an imperative (GMM 421n).

And

> The principle that makes certain actions a duty is a practical law. Th rule that the agent himself makes his principle on subjective grounds is called his *maxim*. Thus different men can have quite different maxims with regard to the same law (MM 224).

In the first place, maxims and laws are distinguished here in terms of ob-objectivity (laws) and subjectivity (maxims). And objectivity is established not only by universality but also by necessity—that is, the determination of the will by laws and by maxims must differ with respect to *modality* as well as with respect to quantity. Second, the subjectivity of maxims is linked here with the fact that maxims are rules "determined by reason in accordance with the conditions of the subject." Kant does not say that only immoral maxims are so determined; rather, he implies that maxims *as such* are so determined. Third, maxims are said to be *chosen*, whereas laws are *imposed* (practical obligation for us is necessitation). And fourth, maxims are principles on which a person acts (laws are only mediately principles for action; immediately they are principles for maxims).

I think that all of these ways of distinguishing laws from maxims point to an essential difference in the function of the two kinds of principles in willing. And Kant says that explicitly:

> Laws proceed from the Wille—maxims proceed from the Willkür (MM 225).

So the difference between maxims and laws is grounded in the different functions of Wille and Willkür in willing. Kant clarifies these different functions as follows:

> The appetitive power that acts in accordance with concepts, insofar as the ground determining it to action lies in itself and not in the object, is called a power *to act or to refrain from acting at one's discretion.* It is called Willkür when it is joined with consciousness that its action can produce the object; otherwise its act is called a *wish.* The appetitive power whose inner determining ground, and so the liking itself, lies in the subject's reason is called Wille. Wille is therefore the appetitive power viewed not so much (like Willkür) in relation to action as in relation to the grounds determining Willkür to the action ... (MM 212).

So we can distinguish different aspects of the will's functioning under the names Wille and Willkür. And the distinction corresponds to whether we consider the will in relation to its determining grounds in reason or in relation to its object. We can express this distinction in different terms as follows: The will is a faculty of rational causality. If we view the will in its function as Wille we consider it as *rational* causality; if we view it in its function as Willkür we consider it as rational *causality.* Moreover, as a *causal* faculty the will involves both *concepts* of its objects (as effects) and *feeling* for its objects. So when we consider Wille we are concerned with the role *reason* plays in willing, and when we consider Willkür we are concerned with the roles played by practical *understanding* and the faculty of *pleasure and pain.*

It should be noted in passing that (as Beck points out—Beck 1966, 75, 177), in the second Critique Kant is not strictly precise about his use of the *words* Wille and Willkür. But (as Beck also points out—Beck, 1966, 177) the lack of precision boils down to the fact that Kant uses Wille to mean both practical reason (the strict meaning of Wille) and will in general (which includes Willkür). So, for example, in the formulation of the Fundamental Law (30), "the maxim of you Wille" means "the maxim of your will as a whole," not "the maxim of your pure practical reason." The word "Willkür," however, is never used to mean anything but Willkür, so in that respect Kant is quite consistent.

These two faculties represent irreducibly distinct functions of our will, and it is the fact that they cannot be reduced to one another or to a common ground that creates the transcendental problems of maxims versus laws. To see that problem we need to examine the differences of function among these faculties.

Reason's function in general is inference; reason informs us of the presence or absence of systematic unity according to rules. The presence of that unity is self-consistency; its absence is self-contradiction. In themselves (that is, in their concepts) neither the thought of self-consistency nor the thought of self-contradiction implies any determination of the will to act, nor are they associated immediately with any feeling.

The function of desire, however, is precisely to produce an action: A determination of desire is a determination of our causality—to be aware of a desire is to be aware of our will directing itself toward satisfaction of that desire. That awareness occurs through feeling, through a represented pleasure (a longing) or pain (a distaste). So even though desire represents its objects through concepts, its necessitation is sensible.

So desire and reason are *essentially different* faculties with essentially different functions, and even though they cooperate in willing, the necessitation of one cannot be derived analytically from that of the other. That they cooperate at all in willing is in the first place a matter of *experience*, and what experience teaches is that reason's role in willing is limited to systematizing and weighing pleasures.

In that cooperation reason and desire maintain their essentially distinct functions—reason merely draws the consequences of feeling's premisses. (Thus Kant calls reason's function here "analytic" GMM 417.) Correspondingly, what moral obligation reveals is a synthetic fact—namely, a conclusion drawn by reason, from wholly rational premisses, but in the territory of desire. That is, to the purely rational thought of the lawful form of maxims is added a determination of the appetitive powers.

The synthetic character of the moral will-determination rests on the fact that even in their cooperation the two components of willing (reason and appetition) remain essentially distinct and function according to their own separate laws. Reason may determine desire, but in doing so it must function according to the rules of rationality in general. And desire may be determined by reason, but even that determination must conform to the rules of desire.

It is this distinction between the two components of human volition that underlies the distinction between Wille and Willkür: If we focus on the rational determining grounds of choice we consider will as under laws of reason and therefore as Wille (Wille is practical reason); if we focus on choice with respect to actions we consider will as under laws of nature and therefore as Willkür (Willkür is practical understanding as conditioned by practical sensibility).

Thus Wille is will viewed solely with respect to principles of freedom as distinct from those of nature and therefore viewed as being independent of time. Wille really does not act (cf. MM225), any more than reason's function in apperception can be said to be an event: Both are pure formal functionings of reason apart from sensibility and therefore apart from time. Wille is thus concerned only with the pure form of actions (as lawful or not).

Willkür is will viewed with respect to both natural laws and laws of freedom; or, more precisely, Willkür is will viewed as under laws of nature that are subordinated to laws of freedom: To say that Willkür is free is to say not that natural laws do not govern Willkür but that Willkür's causality (which must always be in accordance with natural laws) is also (from a different viewpoint) subject to a higher determining ground. Willkür's determinations are always causal acts. Willkür is thus concerned with the material of actions, and it is so concerned in two respects: as objective material (as effect in the world of experience of a natural causality under the rule of freedom) and as subjective material (as that for the sake of which the action occurs—the action as tied up with sensible determining grounds of pleasure and pain).

But Wille and Willkür are aspects of a single rational faculty of desire, so that in Wille reason is seen as determinative of desire, and in Willkür desire is seen as lawful—as functioning always according to rules (and these rules—which are, at least formally, always products of reason— are always Willkür's immediate determining grounds).

Wille is the appetitive faculty viewed with respect to its determining ground in reason. The immediate determination of the human will is always by rules: The faculty of pleasure and pain is determinable by an object and its subjective effect on us, but "the will is never determined directly by the object and our representation of it; rather, the will is a faculty for making a rule of reason the motive (Bewegursache) for an action" (60). (I take it Kant is using Wille here in the inclusive sense.) The appetitive faculty viewed with respect to its determining grounds in reason is a faculty for determining principles of action in relation to the ground of lawfulness of principles in general. Note that once again pure practical reason is seen as functioning like reason in pure apperception: What reason apperceives is not an object but only the unity of function in its own synthetic activity; and so likewise Wille's immediate reference is only to the lawful form of its own principles. Wille's function is thus to produce a unity of principles by referring them to a common ground in pure reason (the pure form of lawfulness). That common ground is the basis of the moral law, but it is also presupposed even by prudential willing—it is a necessary resupposition of all systematic unity of practical principles, even of systematic unity under a concept of happiness, since it is only by reference to the representation of a lawful whole (a nature in general) that my desires can be brought to systematic unity and that an action can be willed.

Willkür is the appetitive faculty (which functions according to rules) viewed with respect to its *actions*: Its proper sphere is acting, or choosing (so it is inextricably tied up with temporality and therefore with natural causality and sensibility). Willkür presupposes determinate principles of action as given. Its function is either to adopt (or reject) those principles as maxims or, in the case of already adopted maxims, to choose (or reject) an action. In either case its activity is the synthetic linking of a given rule with a given determination of the appetitive faculty. For example, to adopt the maxim of telling the truth means to unite that rule with my own subjective conditions of willing—whether that be by representing to myself the causal connection between lying and the dangers of being caught in a lie, by connecting truth-telling with the feeling of virtuous superiority that it produces in me, or by acknowledging the necessity of the principle as a law of freedom; and to choose an action on the basis of that principle, once it has been adopted as a maxim, means to use the rule to produce a particular will-determination (e.g., not to tell this lie) from a more general but actual will-determination (not to lie at all)— where by "will-determination" we mean a causal setting of the faculty of desire. In either case Willkür unites a principle as a rule of reason with subjective conditions (actual will-determinations as determinations of a faculty of natural causality). The result is the choice of an action or of a maxim. So maxims are principles not simply as rules of reason but as rules under conditions of natural causality (i.e., they are principles made necessary not solely by their rational form but also by their connection with natural causes and therefore with natural lawfulness). It is really with the choice of maxims (rather than the choice of actions) that we are concerned in a critique of practical reason in general, since it is on the level of the choice of maxims that the questions of moral philosophy arise in full force.

What is essential to this understanding of Willkür is the idea that choice always involves a synthetic relationship between reason and desire: For a maxim to be chosen means that it is in some way linked to subjective conditions (i.e., to the subject's natural causality and its sensible determining grounds in feeling). If the maxim is chosen prudentially, then the linking to natural grounds of determination is in the form of representing a pleasurable object as grounding the maxim; in that case the link with sensibility provides the "motive force" for the principle. If the maxim is chosen morally, sensibility does not provide a motive force: We can never expect to like to do the good; but, on the other hand, the moral law is its own incentive—we need no further "push." But sensible determining grounds are always present at least as opposition: The fact that the moral law is itself the incentive for the adoption of moral maxims does not mean that sensibility need not be taken into account. Moral maxims must still be *chosen*—they must still be actively adopted into my faculty of desire as *my* causal principles. For that purpose they must be linked to sensibility, not as grounded in pleasure but as the supreme source of determinability of sensibility, to which sensuous pleasure is a priori subordinated.

Willkür is a faculty of natural causality. It always acts in time and thus is always subject to laws of nature. This subjection to laws of nature is manifested in the fact that Willkür always has an object (even though that object may not be its determining ground) represented as an effect of Willkür's causality. And Willkür is always an appetitive faculty: Its objects are always represented as standing in some relation to pleasure and pain (even though that relation may not determine the choice but may, rather, be determined *by* the choice). So no principle can become my maxim for acting except insofar as it stands in some determinate relation to these subjective conditions: Any principle that I adopt must fulfill the requirements of maxims in general, which conditions are imposed by practical understanding and sensibility. The requirement imposed by practical understanding is that every maxim involves the representation of an effect (an object); and the requirement of sensibility is that every maxim must contain a determination of the faculty of pleasure and pain (an incentive).

Now our aim in introducing the distinction between Wille and Willkür in the first place was to clarify the distinction between laws and maxims and, further, to see in what way laws can become maxims or maxims can be willed as at the same time laws. Our original clue was Kant's statement that "laws proceed from Wille, maxims proceed from Willkür" (MM225), and our analysis of Wille and Willkür aimed at exhibiting them as functions of separate faculties (reason, on the one hand, and understanding and sensibility, on the other).

So now we can see better how laws and maxims are *distinct*: Laws, as products of Wille, are principles of the appetitive faculty framed with reference only to their relation to a (formal) systematic unity of rational principles. They are universal and necessary precisely because they are not grounded in any determinate physical reality. Since they are not so grounded—not tied to any particular will-determination—they are not restricted to the particular sensible conditions (of pleasure and pain) that would necessarily be tied up with the ground of such a will-determination: They are not rules for a particular will but rather for will as such.

Maxims are principles functioning as principles of real actions; that is, they are principles that have been linked to our natural causality and sensibility and thus placed in a determinate relationship to the physical world (to real existence) through the subject's causal agency. (This is why maxims are always *my own* and *chosen* and have their proper function only in *acting*.) But the determinate reference to existence is always by reference to sensibility as subjective conditions (viz., of pleasure and pain). So principles adopted as maxims, by gaining concrete objective reference to physical reality, lose their practical universality and necessity. They are linked to grounds of *physical* necessity (ends as natural causes), which are, from the practical viewpoint, no matter what role they play in willing, subjective and *contingent*. A principle cannot be both a maxim (a chosen principle) and a law at the same time and in precisely the same respect. Even though the principle might be a universalizable one (e.g., not lying), insofar as I have chosen it as *my* maxim I have adopted it contingently (through a reference to subjective conditions). There thus seems to be no way that the principle can remain simply necessary and at the same time be *my* maxim.

Maxims as Laws

We have seen that the command that maxims be willed as at the same time laws cannot mean that maxims should be replaced with laws in our willing. That replacement is impossible; for it to be possible would mean that our will would become an infinite will that did not merely *cause* its objects but actually *created* them, so that the laws of "nature" of the objects would be identical to the laws of their production by our will. That is not possible for a finite will, which is always conditioned by a natural necessity that is, from the viewpoint of practical reason, contingent and yet not to be done away with. So the willing of maxims as laws must involve a more complicated process than simple replacement.

The fact that maxims always express a natural causality (and thus refer to experience) appears on the level of practical "epistemology" as the fact that maxims always refer to objects as effects (that is, that maxims are products of practical understanding and so presuppose concepts of effects as cause of the existence of those effects) and the fact that those effects are always represented as conditioned by a reference to sensibility (to pleasure and pain). (These two features of maxims are what I refer to elsewhere as the objective and subjective material of maxims.)

If these features of maxims are ineradicable, then the moral law, rather than replacing them, must adapt itself to them. That is, moral willing, just as much as prudential willing, must have reference to some object as effect and must involve some determination of sensibility (some "for the sake of which"). The full elucidation of what it means for the moral law to adapt itself to our subjective conditions and of how that is possible involves showing that the lawful form of maxims can determine choice immediately and that pleasure and pain are thereby excluded or outweighed as determining grounds (and it would be necessary to show the consequences of that); but that is the task of the entire Analytic. What we can do here is to show how the formulation of the moral law *already expresses the adaptation of the law to the human will*.

The moral law commands *universally* and *necessarily* (that is, unconditionally), whereas maxims are always particular and are always adopted under conditions of my own subjectivity. The law does not command the elimination of maxims (instead it says "So act that the maxim of your will ..."); rather, it imposes certain conditions upon my maxims and upon my mode of willing them. The requirement of universality can be met if my maxims are chosen in the first place in such a way that, although not themselves willed as *universal* (in which case they would not be maxims), they are *universalizable* - that is, they could hold as laws of nature without contradicting the defining feature of nature as such, namely, its systematic unity and harmony according to laws.

If I chose my maxims in that way I would be obeying a law that said "Act only on maxims that could be universalized, " and my action would be *legal* but not necessarily *moral* (cf. MM 388: " 'So act that the maxim of your will could become a universal law.' Ethics adds only that this principle is to be conceived as the law of *your own will* and not of will in general, which could also be the will of another." It is significant that Beck, in his commentary, paraphrases the moral principle from the *Groundwork* in exactly that way - Beck 173.) So far as juridical duty (legality of actions) is concerned, the adoption of the law into my maxim offers no great difficulties: I need not act on universal laws, but I act on maxims that could be made into universal laws (maxims that are universalizable). But that does not yet give us the moral law.

The command of morality, as opposed to that of juridical duty, is an unconditional command: It commands with *necessity*. (And, incidentally, this provides a clue to Kant's claim, with respect to the categories of freedom, that it is the categories of modality that initiate the transition from categories of practical reason in general to those of morality.) By choosing my maxims to be universalizable I do not eliminate their essential contingency: They are still objects of my choice and so are inevitably linked to conditions imposed by my practical understanding and sensibility. for example, I might adopt universalizable maxims because I think they are most likely to allow me a happy life (by freeing me from conflicts with others, etc.). Or I might adopt them because of my belief in an afterlife in which I will be rewarded for them. In those cases my actions are not moral. So the question is How can actions *ever* be moral, granted that maxims are subjective principles?

The solution is not that subjective conditions be eliminated from maxims but that the moral law determine those subjective conditions, so that morality itself becomes the "content" of my maxim - its willed effect and that for the sake of which the maxim is willed. In that case the moral law is still adopted into my maxim under some condition and is still willed for the sake of some content, but the condition and the content are morality itself and not something that must be sensibly given (on the contrary, the moral content itself determines sensibility). That would mean that in moral willing *two* components must be present: the maxim functioning as maxim (as subjective principle) and therefore as particular and contingent, and the same maxim (or, strictly speaking, the same principle, now *not* functioning as maxim) willed as universal law. This appears most clearly in the formulation of the law as the principle of autonomy given at GMM 440: "Never to choose except in such a way that the maxims of your choice are in the same willing, at the same time, comprehended (mitbegreifen) as universal law."

It is the presence of this second element that makes willing *moral* willing as opposed to merely *legal* willing: a maxim can be willed as in the same volition, at the same time, a law only insofar as the mere lawful form of the maxim (its form of universal lawgiving) is taken as the content of the maxim (that for the sake of which the maxim is chosen). This appears most clearly in the categorical imperative formulated as the moral principle at GMM 447: "An absolutely good will is one whose maxim can always contain *itself* considered as a universal law" (my emphasis). (Paton translates the phrase "contain itself" - perhaps not quite literally, but on this interpretation perfectly correctly - as "have as its content itself.")

Likewise in the "official" formulation of the moral law given in the second Critique (30) - "So act that the maxim of your will could always hold (gelten) at the same time as a principle establishing universal law" - the verb "gelten" must be understood as referring to the activity of a faculty of *evaluation*, not to a merely logical appraisal (which is why, in other formulations, "gelten können" is replaced with "can be willed").

The presence of the "at the same time" (zugleich) is a clue to this interpretation of these formulas: In one and the same act (and not in a causal sequence) principles are functioning in two different ways - as universal and necessary (laws - principles for will as such) and as particular and contingent (maxims - principles for *my* will).

To spell that out further, even in moral willing my maxim is necessarily subject to the conditions of natural causality; in particular that means that the maxim must always have a "material," both objectively (as represented effect of the action the maxim prescribes) and subjectively (as that for the sake of which the action occurs). Those features of a finite will need not include the determining grounds of the will, but they do contain necessary conditions on finite willing: A finite will is a *rationally* determinable *natural* cause. A maxim functioning as a maxim is always the rule of a causal relationship subject to the laws of nature. That causality involves the representation of the existence of an effect that serves as cause for the action that produces the effect. This structure of maxim-willing is irreducible. So if the material is not to be the determining ground of action, the form of the maxim itself must determine the will and become its material - that is, the maxim must be willed for the sake of itself represented as universal law.

What happens in this process is that the maxim, as an expression of a natural lawfulness, is (practically) subordinated to (willed for the sake of) a principle that can only be grounded in freedom. That is, in moral action the will is determined by the representation of the subordination of natural necessity to the necessity of a realm of freedom. In fact, the material realm is seen as having its *ground* in the realm of freedom.

Our results can be summarized as follows: (1) Maxims and laws are irreducibly different (they are products of different faculties). (2) Therefore the willing of maxims as laws must be a complex operation involving two distinct components, viz., (a) the willing of a principle as maxim (that is, as subjective and contingent—i.e., subject to natural laws as conditions) and (b) the willing of the same principle as universal law. And

(3) these two components must be willed together in a relationship of practical subordination—i.e., the willing of the principle as maxim must be for the sake of the principle willed as universal law.

In no other way, I think, can we make sense out of the literal wording of all the various formulations of the moral law. (And it can also be seen that this interpretation does away with Beck's difficulty about the relative inclusiveness of the terms "maxim," "law," and "principle": Both maxims and laws are—as Kant says—kinds of principles; but they differ in the way they function in willing, and that difference is essential to their *being* maxims and laws, respectively.)

These conclusions can be seen to be in keeping with our general theses that the argument in the Analytic can only be understood in terms of the interrelations of distinct faculties and that the aim of the argument is to establish the necessary subordination of sensible determining grounds of the will to rational determining grounds. But it should also be clearer now how important it is that Kant begins with establishing a realm of freedom: Practical laws have application only with respect to maxims—that is, *laws of freedom are laws for rules of natural causality*: The entire realm of nature is subordinate to the realm of freedom, and the focal point of that subordination is our maxims.

NOTES

1. For an explanation of my method of citing references, see the Preface, pp. iif.

2. The fact that it is the Deduction that is taken as the model for transcendental arguments points to a general confusion that runs throughout the literature—namely, the identification of a transcendent argument with a transcendental deduction. There has been almost no attempt to distinguish the two, and, indeed, usually the need for distinguishing them is not even recognized. I think it would be extremely useful to try to discover whether, for example, a deduction is a particular *kind* of transcendental argument, a particular *part* of a transcendental argument, or something else. I have not explicitly addressed that question, but in Chapter 8 I offer some tentative suggestions based on our results.

3. Here and throughout I use the word "prove" loosely. Kant has much to say on the kinds of proof and the kinds of certainty that are possible in different areas of knowledge (cf. KrV A712/B740 ff.), but I have for the most part not strictly adhered to his terminology. Instead I use the terms "proof" and "argument" more or less interchangeably.

4. This formulation has its roots in Henrich's "two-steps-in-one-proof" structure proposed for the B-edition deduction of the first Critique, and that, in turn, was developed with reference to the "that/how" and "objective/subjective" structures formulated by Adickes and Paton and by de Vleeschauwer, respectively (see Henrich, 1969, 642 ff. and references 4 and 5 cited there). But the "must/can" formulation was originated by John Wetlaufer (private communication), and it is to him that I am indebted for its use. It might at first seem strange to propose an argument-structure in which necessity is proved first and possibility second (the traditional line of reasoning being that necessity implies possibility); but it must be kept in mind that the necessity in question is the necessity of consequences logically deducible from a given determination of our conceptional faculties, whereas any further determination of a concept

(insofar as it lays claim to being knowledge) involves at least an implicit reference to our sensible faculties, and the conditions of the latter cannot he analytically derived from those of the former.

5. This division of steps relies heavily upon Henrich's division (Henrich, 1969), but it also changes somewhat the interpretation of the principle of division. I think the two approaches are not incompatible, but to show that would require a thorough investigation of the relation between his "two-steps-in-one-proof" structure and the "must/can" structure, which would carry us beyond the scope of this enquiry into an analysis of the first Critique.

6. I have argued elsewhere that this is the truly decisive difference between the argument of the second Critique and that of Chapter III of the *Groundwork*—see my article "The Transcendental Argument in Kant's *Groundwork of the Metaphysic of Morals.*"

7. For a fuller discussion of the categories and the importance of their generality, see my article "Kant's Categories of Practical Reason as Such."

8. That Beck holds to the idea of there being some sort of deduction of the moral law is shown in the first place by his division of his *Commentary* into a "metaphysical deduction" of the moral law (Beck 109—125) and a "transcendental deduction" of the law (Beck actually refers to the "moral principle" rather than to the moral law in the latter section, but by the moral principle he apparently means the moral law). It is also indicated by passages like these: "...while the moral law serves as a ground for the deduction of freedom, the concept of freedom is made to serve also as the 'credential' of the moral law" (Beck, 174); and

> What, we may ask at the end of this circuitous route, has been gained for the principle of pure practical reason? The fundamental principle, already asserted as a "fact", is not left a naked and isolated assertion or an assertion surrounded by a closed, circular, and empty system. It is supported in that it is precisely of the form required if the dialectic of theoretical reason is not to be irresolvable (Beck, 175).

It is true that Kant says (at 47—8) that the deduction provides a "credential" for the moral law; but it is also clear that that is not the main point of the deduction, and to emphasize that point is to obscure the real import of the deduction.

9. All references to Beck in this Appendix are to his *Commentary* , so I have omitted the year of publication from citations.

BIBLIOGRAPHY

English Editions of Works by Kant Cited in Text

Critique of Judgment, translated by James Creed Meredith, Oxford
   University Press, 1973.

Critique of Practical Reason, translated by Lewis White Beck,
   Bobbs-Merrill, Liberal Arts Press, 1956.

Critique of Pure Reason, translated by Norman Kemp Smith, St. Martin's
   Press, 1965.

Doctrine of Virtue, Part II of the Metaphysic of Morals, translated by
   Mary J. Gregor, Harper and Row, 1964.

First Introduction to the Critique of Judgment, translated by James
   Haden, Bobbs-Merrill, 1965.

Groundwork of the Metaphysic of Morals, translated by H. J. Paton,
   Harper Torchbooks, 1964.

*Kant's Critique of Practical Reason and Other Works on the Theory of
   Ethics*, translated by Thomas Kingsmill Abbott, Longmans, 1963.

Lectures on Ethics, translated by Louis Infield, Harper Torchbooks,
   1963.

Logic, translated by Robert Hartman and Wolfgang Schwarz, The Library
   of Liberal Arts, Bobbs-Merrill, 1974.

Religion within the Limits of Reason Alone, translated by Theodore
   M. Greene and Hoyt H. Hudson, Harper Torchbooks, 1960.

Works by Other Authors

Angelleli, Ignacio (1972). "On the Origins of Kant's 'Transcendental.' "
   Kant-Studien 63, 117.

Beck, Lewis White (1965). *Studies in the Philosophy of Kant*. Bobbs-
   Merrill, Indianapolis.

——(1966). *A Commentary on Kant's Critique of Practical Reason*.
   Phoenix Books, Chicago.

Benton, Robert J. (1978). "The Transcendental Argument in Kant's
    Groundwork of the Metaphysic of Morals." *Journal of Value Inquiry*
    (to be published).

---(1978). "Kant's Categories of Practical Reason as such." (to be
    published).

Bübner, Rüdiger (1975). "Kant, Transcendental Argument, and the
    Problem of Deduction." *Review of Metaphysics* XXVIII, 453.

Cassirer, Ernst (1967). "Kant and the Problem of Metaphysics," in
    Kant: Disputed Questions, Moltke Gram, ed. Quadrangle Books,
    Chicago.

Crawford, Patricia (1963). "Kant's Theory of Philosophical Proof."
    Kant-Studien 54, 257.

de Vleeschauwer, H. J. (1937). *La déduction transcendentale dans l'oeuvr*
    de Kant, Vol. 3, *La déduction transcendentale de 1787 jusqu'à*
    l'Opus Postumum, pp. 299–338. Librairie Ernest Leroux, Paris.

Gram, Moltke S. (1971). "Transcendental Arguments." *Nous* 5, 15.

---(1973). "Categories and Transcendental Arguments." *Man and World*
    6, 252.

---(1974). "Must Transcendental Arguments be Spurious?" *Kant-Studien*
    65, 304.

---(1975). "Must We Revisit Transcendental Arguments?" *Journal of*
    Philosophy LXXII.

Hartmann, Klaus (1967). "On Taking the Transcendental Turn."
    Review of Metaphysics XX, 223.

Heidegger, Martin (1962). *Kant and the Problem of Metaphysics.*
    Indiana University Press, Bloomington, Indiana.

Henrich, Dieter (1960). "Der Begriff der sittlichen Einsicht und Kants
    Lehre vom Faktum der Vernunft," in *Die Gegenwart der Griechen*
    im neueren Denken. J. C. B. Mohr (Paul Siebeck), Tübingen.

---(1969). "The Proof-Structure of Kant's Transcendental Deduction."
    Review of Metaphysics XXII, 640.

Hinske, Norbert (1973). "Kants Begriff des Transzendentalen und die Problematik seiner Begriffsgeschichte." *Kant-Studien* 64, 56.

Hintikka, Jaakko (1972). "Transcendental Arguments: Genuine and Spurious." *Nous* 6, 274.

Kelley, George Armstrong (1969). "The Structure and Spirit of Legality in Kant." *Journal of Politics* 31, 513.

Körner, Stephen (1955). *Kant*. Penguin Books, Baltimore, Maryland.

---(1966). "Transcendental Tendencies in Recent Philosophy." *Journal of Philosophy* 63, 19.

---(1967). "The Impossibility of Transcendental Deductions." *Monist* 51, 317.

Muck, Otto (1969). "The Logical Structure of Transcendental Method." *International Philosophical Quarterly*, 9, 342.

Paton, H. J. (1967). *The Categorical Imperative*. Harper Torchbook, New York.

Rosenberg, Jay F. (1975). "Transcendental Arguments Revisited." *Journal of Philosophy LXXII*.

Schaper, Eva (1972). "Arguing Transcendentally." *Kant-Studien* 63, 101.

Schrader, George (1964). "Basic Problems of Philosophical Ethics." *Archiv für Geschichte der Philosophie* 46, 102.

Silber, John R. (1959a). "Kant's Conception of the Highest Good as Immanent and Transcendent." *Philosophical Review* 68, 469.

---(1959b). "The Copernican Revolution in Ethics: The Good Reexamined." *Kant-Studien* 51, 85.

---(1959c). "The Context of Kant's Ethical Thought." *Philosophical Quarterly* 9, 193 and 309.

---(1960). "The Ethical Significance of Kant's *Religion*," Introductory essay in *Religion within the Limits of Reason Alone*, translated by Greene and Hudson. Harper Torchbooks, New York.

---(1960/1961). "Die Analyse des Pflicht- und Schuld-Erlebnisses bei Kant und Freud." *Kant-Studien* 52, 295.

---(1962—63). "The Importance of the Highest Good in Kant's Ethics."
Ethics 73, 179.

---(1966). "Der Schematismus der Praktischen Vernunft." *Kant-Studien*
56, 253.

---(1974). "Procedural Formalism in Kant's Ethics." *Review of
Metaphysics XXVII*, 197.

Stine, William (1972). "Transcendental Arguments." *Metaphilosophy*
3, 43.

Stroud, Barry (1968). "Transcendental Arguments." *Journal of
Philosophy* 65, 251.

Watt, A. J. (1968). "Transcendental Arguments and Moral Principles."
Philosophical Quarterly 25, 40.

Wetlaufer, John (1975). "On the Transcendental Deduction: Some
Problems of Interpretation and Elements of a New Reading."
Graduate Faculty Philosophy Journal 5, 113.

Wilkerson, T. E. (1970). "Transcendental Arguments." *Philosophical
Quarterly* 20, 200.

Wood, Allen W. (1970). *Kant's Moral Religion*. Cornell University
Press, Ithaca.